THE FUTURE ON SCREEN

sisomo

CREATING EMOTIONAL CONNECTIONS IN THE MARKET WITH SIGHT, SOUND AND MOTION

KEVIN ROBERTS

CEO WORLDWIDE, SAATCHI & SAATCHI, IDEAS COMPANY

powerHouse Books New York, NY

LOST

I love *Lost*! I've watched every episode at least twice. I'll spend days trying to figure out what's going on. It's so addictive to watch because it feels like I'm right there on the island with them. I also get to see each character's back story, so I know each of them better than they know each other. Why are they being chased by polar bears? Who is that French woman? What's under the hatch? Maybe I'll never find out, but I'll be glued to my screen until the end of the last episode.

Toby, Australia

BRAVO

For bringing this channel to TV and for opening my heart to love more beauty, music, humor and truth about life. When Cirque du Soleil came on Bravo, I went out and bought a big screen, surround sound TV to enjoy the passion, colors and music.

Linda, United States

PLACEBO

Placebo reinvented the whole idea of what music actually is. Placebo has a sound like no other. It makes my heart pound and my blood boil. They are just so totally different. With a sound like theirs, sometimes it's easy for me to forget that they are just mere human beings.

Ludovica, Italy

BLIZZARD ENTERTAINMENT

The gaming company that has consistently produced hit after hit with games like *Warcraft*, *Starcraft* and *Diablo*. Gamers like me anticipate their releases for years, and sign up in the tens of thousands for the chance to test a single game. Mention the name Blizzard in a forum and you'll get gamers remembering some of their best gameplay moments. Lovemark worthy? Of course.

Vysion, United States

PETER JACKSON

Everyone's favorite director, and for good reason. PJ is brilliant. Only he could take J.R.R. Tolkien's beautiful works of literature and turn them into works of film just as beautiful. We salute you, Peter!

Penni, United States

TIMES SQUARE, NEW YORK

Whether you're there at night or during the day, there's nothing cooler than Times Square. Looking up at those huge screens gives you hope for the future. You know that despite all our hang-ups and fears and worries, we're still making progress, and that one day we'll be living in a wired-up utopia, communicating with and understanding people half a world away through our screens. Times Square is a symbol of a smaller, closer world.

J.C., China

XBOX

That somewhat alien but warm green glow from inside my entertainment center, the sound as the processor fan spins up, and then the television screen lighting up. Oh, many a late night has been wasted with my trusty Xbox. Whether we were hunting another "Master Sarge" or were in upper Seattle looking for some church, the 'box has always been there for me.

Ward, United States

SONAR 4

When I was younger, I never dreamt I could do the things that I'm now doing with this software. I would have needed tens of thousands of dollars to do the same things in a studio, and some of the things that SONAR enables were not even possible back then. It extends my creativity and makes realizing my dreams possible.

Mao, United States

OLYMPIC GAMES

I love the Olympic Games. On TV, we get a living history of the host country, along with some of their customs. I'm glued every evening watching all of the events. And there ARE plenty of surprises. If the US doesn't have anyone left in a competition, sometimes there is a favorite from another country, like Ana from Mexico—a favorite in track and field, who won silver. And a Canadian won silver in men's springboard diving. The list could go on and on. That's why I love watching the Olympics.

Holly, United States

APPLE'S IPOD

iPod is the best thing since Sony's Walkman. With a color screen and video playback it might be even greater, maybe. But I love it anyway. Period.

Yasin, Indonesia

FEEDDEMON

My morning ritual: cup of coffee, sit at the computer, start up FeedDemon. FeedDemon gives me up-to-the-minute news about the things I care about, and nothing else. What's more intimate than that? Interesting links, news and podcasts served fresh each morning, ready for me to peruse or trash or file away for a later date. How long before we get video this way too? Can't wait. FeedDemon's like a part of me. It's my connection to the rest of the world.

Alicia, Argentina

SHAH RUKH KHAN

It goes without saying that Shah Rukh Khan is the best thing to have happened to Hindi cinema. He is a phenomenon whose influence goes far beyond a mere screen presence. For me and my family, he has been a constant source of pleasure and inspiration. He is the reason we watch Hindi films and I am sure there are many more like us. May he continue to shine in millions of hearts for generations to come. He is an actor par excellence. God bless him.

Shaheen, United States

CONTENTS

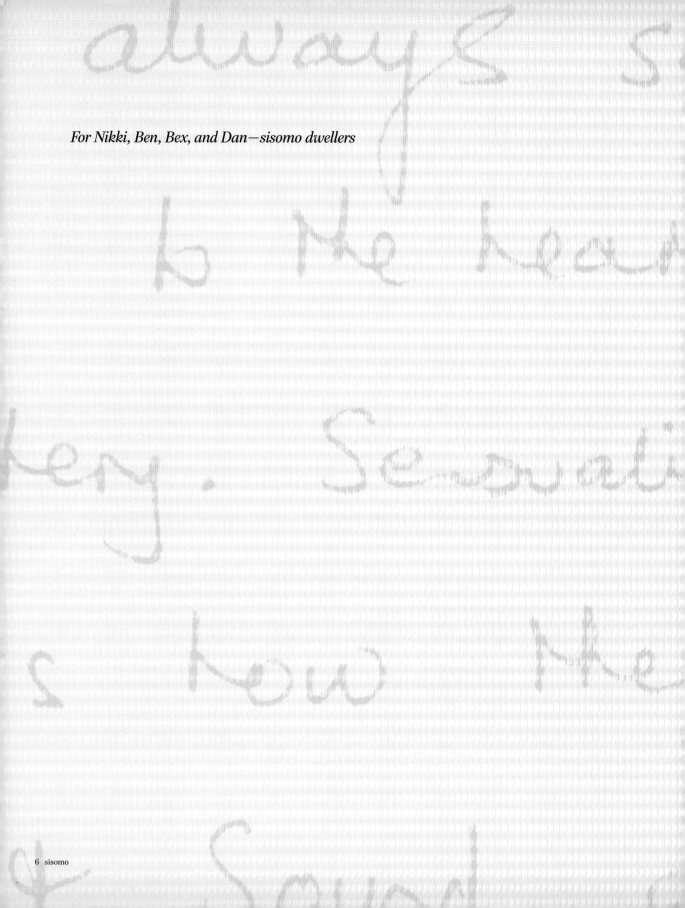

For Nikki, Ben, Bex, and Dan—sisomo dwellers

I've always said there are three
keys to the hearts of consumers.
Mystery, Sensuality and Intimacy.
Here's how they come alive.
Sight, Sound and Motion.

Kevin Roberts, CEO Worldwide, Saatchi & Saatchi

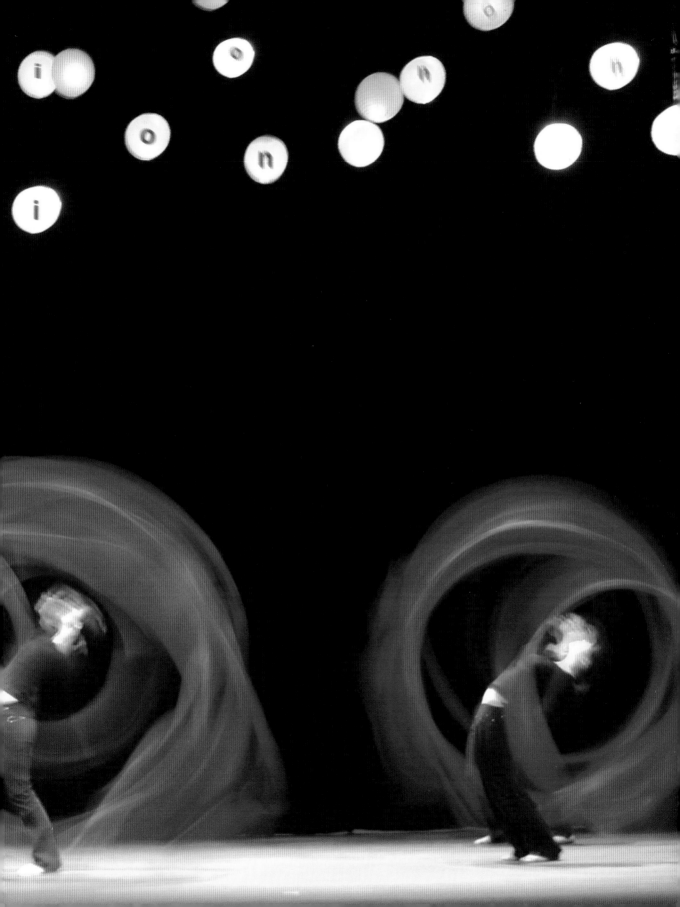

"sisomo demystifies technology and unleashes its creative potential."

CHAPTER 1

SISOMO: THE FUTURE ON SCREEN

People have always loved watching screens. We have all felt the attraction. In the early days of television, before we got a set of our own, I remember the fascination of televisions on display in store windows. Like everyone else, I'd stand on the street gazing in at the magic of the moving images and feel the future had arrived.

We are now living in that future. The Screen Age. Screens for informing, entertaining, communicating, connecting, transacting, controlling. Screens for every need and purpose. And as these screens spread everywhere in our lives, it is becoming clear that using them with skill and creativity is the solution to the key communications and marketing challenges of our time.

Reaching today's consumers is a challenge up there with traveling to Mars. Consumers are now savvy activists wired into the most dense communications networks the world has ever known. These new consumers are well-informed, critical and full of ideas to connect and be connected, choose and be chosen, download and upload.

In the face of the amazing possibilities technology offers, consumers have never lost their overwhelming desire for simplicity.

It is this desire that inspired sisomo.

New ideas need new words. sisomo is a new word for something so familiar we take it for granted. Sight, Sound and Motion on screen.

Using the simplicity of emotion, Lovemarks took branding away from the marketers and put it into the hands of consumers.

Using the simplicity of Sight, Sound and Motion, sisomo is about the same transfer of control. It takes power from the traditional sisomo industries of production and distribution and puts it in the hands of consumers everywhere.

sisomo and Lovemarks are the new language of the twenty-first century market.

Together, I believe, they will allow us to think with our hearts and feel with our brains. Now we can keep it simple *and* keep it emotional.

With Lovemarks we knew there were three keys to the heart: Mystery, Sensuality and Intimacy. Here's how they come alive:

Sight, Sound and Motion.

Sight, Sound and Motion are the most potent ingredients for compelling communications. Humans love excitement. They revel in shape and color. They are passionate about music. They are attracted by movement.

The right side of the brain is finding new respectability in the twenty-first century. Creativity, empathy, inspiration and emotional context have new value as our analytical skills struggle to cope with the information deluge.

Thank goodness. I say, let's call it the sisomo brain!

> "If you can't deal with screen language, you aren't literate."
>
> *John Seely Brown*

THE CONVERGENCE EQUATION

For well over a decade, the convergence of technologies has been an aspiration and a catch-cry. Converge or be converged!

We have gone from the straightforward combination of television-like visuals and computers in the cautious world of "multimedia" to today's clamorous marketplace. Computers have become massively connected through the Internet. Television has been transformed by the interplay of broadcast, cable, wireless, satellite and DVRs. And the convergence equation has been complicated by mobile phones, gaming systems and the rest of the digital pack.

Business has seen convergence either as a brilliant future or a looming threat, as more and more players elbow their way in.

Computer companies, telecommunications companies and consumer electronics manufacturers are having new conversations with the television networks, the cable guys and online companies, and they are all eyeing up the new interaction of Madison and Vine.

The new world convergence is creating is still immature and tough to get a grip on. Described in technical terms and obscured by confusing acronyms, it is fueled more by industry competition than by consumer need, let alone delight.

We cannot allow the multiplicity of possibilities to drag us into complexity. Saatchi & Saatchi works with many of the leading producers of sisomo experiences on television and phones, online and in-store. We have all learned that trying to control the growing complexity of technology is a waste of time. And we all know that to survive, we have to keep a stake in it somewhere.

Our key to this puzzle is simple. sisomo is the true energy of the convergence equation, not the latest chips or highest-definition screens. sisomo gives purpose and clarity to what we have to do next.

EMOTIONAL CONNECTIONS

Let's step back. For all the furor about convergence, and new technologies and opportunities, we need to converge on one idea: making emotional connections with people.

This is the convergence that matters because it is focused on what consumers need and desire, and not on what the technology does best.

We believe that looking at technology convergence through the eyes of consumers gives you the smart, long-term view. The place to start is with the senses, the point where any experience of the world is created.

> "Get on top of technology before technology is on top of you." *Prince*

The mastery of sisomo made television one of the most inspiring inventions of the twentieth century, and the greatest selling medium invented so far.

But where television was once the master of sisomo, today we can choose from a family of sisomo-savvy screens that are welcoming new members at extraordinary speed.

And these screens are not confined to the living room. They have moved out into the world and taken sisomo with them. On computers, mobile phones, PDAs, in-store displays and consoles, in sports stadiums, on the sides of buildings and out of the corner of the eye, wherever we go, screens deliver sisomo 24 hours a day.

SISOMO IS WHAT MAKES THE IMAGES YOU SEE ON THE SCREEN EMOTIONALLY COMPELLING

In passing, you'll notice I call what are often known as cell phones, mobile phones. It has always seemed weird to me that, in an age that focuses so intensely on consumers, the coolest consumer gadgets are so often named after a technical process. I'm for calling them what they are. Mobiles. Phones that travel at the beck and call of their owners, who live and work in a mobile age.

THE FAMILY OF SCREENS

The digital revolution has arrived. sisomo on the new family of screens offers the biggest and most exciting opportunity to connect with consumers since television first burst into the room.

What holds our new wealth of possibilities together is the screen and what brings the screen to life is sisomo. A direct and emotional connection to consumers that can inspire fresh ideas, new partnerships, innovative business models and a way to cut through the clutter.

What does this mean for television? The rumor that television is dead is false. In emerging markets, television offers the same excitement and opportunities that riveted Americans in the 1950s. And wherever television is treated like a comfortable pair of slippers, here comes sisomo to transform it into dancing shoes. Viewers want to skip through whatever bores them. sisomo can up the entertainment, the excitement and the emotion so they don't want to miss a minute.

And now the experience is being energized and amplified by the screen in-store, in cars, in kiosks and on mobile phones. Screens used to give us information and drive transactions, but inspired by sisomo, they can now touch emotions through stories and experiences.

Nowhere does this emotional relationship between screen and consumer offer more opportunities than in-store. The shopping experience is being transformed. It is no big secret that consumers are emotional beings. For instance, we know that in supermarkets up to 80 percent of all brand decisions are made in-store. We don't tick items off a list. We respond emotionally to the experience of shopping. Nowhere does this emotional relationship between screen and consumer offer more opportunities than in-store.

THE SEAMLESS WOW!

You can feel its inspiration everywhere. Start with this book. We have a new story to tell about screens and sisomo. Strategic, responsive and inclusive.

The screen is the new marketplace for great ideas, but like any marketplace, it is only as good as what flows through it. Products, services, ideas, information, inspirations.

Making great content for screens is one of the most exciting creative opportunities of the coming decades. If you have kids, point them in this direction. If you are just starting out, start at sisomo and keep moving. Entrepreneurs, idealists, designers and artists can all define new careers inspired by sisomo. Energize your business by asking, "How do we become more sisomo?"

As composer John Cage told us, "I can't understand why people are frightened of new ideas. I'm frightened of the old ones."

The combination of Sight, Sound and Motion has always been a compelling attraction.

CHAPTER 2

SISOMOMENTS

From the first screening of *The Jazz Singer* to the launch of *Halo 2*, sisomo's take-up on screen has been meteoric. It's hard to believe that when television was first introduced, many people thought it had a limited life-span.

British newspaper publisher C.P. Scott sneered, "Television? The word is half Latin and half Greek. No good can come of it."

Even before television's introduction, early inventors like John Logie Baird were dogged by suspicion.

"For God's sake, go down to reception and get rid of a lunatic who's down there. He says he's got a machine for seeing by wireless! Watch him—he may have a razor on him." This was the editor of London's *Daily Express*, refusing to see Baird in 1925.

Why is it that some of the ideas with the greatest emotional potential are the hardest for us to grasp?

But you can't keep good sisomo down, as this fast track through sisomo's journey from the movie screen to the mobile screen shows.

WALK THE WALK...

When audiences sit down to enjoy the feature *Don Juan* in 1926, none of them know they are attending the first sisomoment in the world. They may have already seen silent movies with piano accompaniment—sisomo-lite—but for the first time, *Don Juan* integrates music and sound effects with the action on screen.

sisomo apparently also inspires love. Reviews are quick to observe that the great Lionel Barrymore recorded the most kisses ever seen in a single film, embracing his co-stars Mary Astor and Estelle Taylor 127 times!

...AND TALK THE TALK

If *Don Juan* marks the birth of sisomo, sisomo takes a giant step a year later when *The Jazz Singer* adds synchronized voices.

And what did Al Jolson, the first voice of sisomo, have to say for himself?

"Wait a minute! Wait a minute! You ain't heard nothin' yet. Wait a minute, I tell ya, you ain't heard nothin'! Do you wanna hear 'Toot, Toot, Tootsie!'? All right, hold on, hold on. (*To the band leader*) Lou, listen. Play 'Toot, Toot, Tootsie!' Three choruses, you understand. In the third chorus I whistle. Now give it to 'em hard and heavy. Go right ahead!"

Animated cartoons will take another year to go sisomo with Walt Disney's *Steamboat Willie* in 1928. Willie's sisomoment was (in Walt's own voice) "Hotdogs! Hotdogs!" Now you know.

"Ginger Rogers did everything Fred Astaire did, but she did it backwards and in high heels."

Anonymous

FIRST daily television broadcast—the BBC in 1936.

FIRST televised sporting event—the 1936 Olympics broadcast to a limited number of sets in Germany.

"There's a good deal in common between the mind's eye and the TV screen, and though the TV set has all too often been the boob tube, it could be, it can be, the box of dreams."

Ursula K. Le Guin

FIRST television commercial—for Bulova clocks—broadcast in New York between a Dodgers and Phillies game in 1941.

CLEANING UP WITH SOAPS

In 1950, Procter & Gamble extend their sponsorship of radio soap operas onto television. The first televised US soap opera was the P&G-sponsored *The First Hundred Years*. Other great P&G television soaps have survived to this day, including *Guiding Light* and the second-longest-running US soap, *As the World Turns*. It was this show that gave Meg Ryan and Julianne Moore their first screen breaks.

HOT SHOTS

Western fever strikes 1950s television with *Maverick*, *Lawman* and the start of the 50-year run of *Gunsmoke*.

"Country music has three chords and the truth."

Harlan Howard

FIRST color television broadcast in the United States in 1951.

FIRST commercial in color featuring Castro Decorators in 1954.

I GOT GAME

FIRST video game, *Tennis for Two*, is created by William Higinbotham in 1958.

FIRST time a helicopter is used for television news—sent up by KTLA Channel 5 in Los Angeles in 1958.

FIRST couple to be shown together in the same bed on prime time is Wilma and Fred Flintstone in 1960.

FIRST instant replay—Army-Navy football game; first slow-motion playback—The World Series of Skiing in Vail, Colorado, in 1967.

GO TO HELL

In 1968, *Star Trek* broadcasts the first spoken use of the word "hell" on television. Check out the *The City on the Edge Forever* episode and watch William Shatner say, "Let's get the hell out of here."

OVER THE MOON

Television is right there in 1969 when Neil Armstrong takes the first small step on the moon. More than 500 million people share the moment on screens around the world.

CUT AND PRINT

The standard length of a television commercial drops from 60 seconds to 30 seconds in 1971.

FIRST home-use video cassette recorder—launched in 1972.

GUESS WHERE I'M CALLING FROM

The statement may be apocryphal, but the first portable mobile phone call made by Dr. Martin Cooper of Motorola still reverberates. From a research idea in 1973 to projections of 3 billion users by 2010, mobile screens are transforming communications, gaming and marketing. And they're just getting started. Emerging markets are leapfrogging to explosive growth, with the number of mobile phone users in 2005 reaching 358 million in China and 82 million in Africa.

THE THRILLER IN MANILA

A satellite link brings the 1975 Ali-Frazier fight to cable and launches HBO, with Ali playing "dope on a rope" before his spectacular win.

FIRST music video—*Bohemian Rhapsody* by Queen in 1975.

"When a man is out of sight, it is not too long before he is out of mind."

Victor Hugo

FIRST reported drop in the number of people watching television since its introduction is noted by a Roper study in 1977.

MUSIC TELEVISION

With supreme irony, MTV launches in 1981 with the British group, The Buggles, performing *Video Killed the Radio Star*.

"If you can walk, you can dance. If you can talk, you can sing."

Zimbabwean proverb

HALF-TIME

Apple launches the Macintosh computer at the 1984 Super Bowl and inspires the imaginations of millions. The 60-second commercial puts screens in the spotlight as a young woman wielding a sledge-hammer smashes the image of "Big Brother." For the record, the actor was Anya Major.

"Today we celebrate the first glorious anniversary of the Information Purification Directives. We have created, for the first time in all history, a garden of pure ideology. Where each worker may bloom secure from the pests of contradictory and confusing truths. Our Unification of Thoughts is more powerful a weapon than any fleet or army on earth. We are one people, with one will, one resolve, one cause. Our enemies shall talk themselves to death and we will bury them with their own confusion. We shall prevail!"
Script for Chiat/Day's Apple Computer 1984 commercial, written by Steve Hayden and directed by Ridley Scott

SO, WHAT'S NEW?

The first website goes online on August 6, 1991 at http://info.cern.ch/. Built by Tim Berners-Lee, the site looks ahead to: "What's New In '92."

CUT TO THE CHASE

It's 1994, and 95 million viewers watch O.J. Simpson flee police on a Los Angeles freeway. In real time.

LET YOUR FINGERS DO THE SHOPPING

Starting with Pizza Hut's first tests of online ordering in Santa Cruz in 1994, online shopping becomes part of life in the United States, accounting for 6.5 percent of total retail sales by 2004.

THE TOYS ARE BACK IN TOWN

In 1995, Buzz Lightyear and Sheriff Woody star in the first digital feature film, *Toy Story*. The film was directed by John Lasseter and created by Pixar Animation Studios, founded by Steve Jobs and Ed Catmull.

WHAT'S IN A NAME?

Jorn Barger first uses the word, *weblog*, in 1997. Two years later it is shortened to the sexier *blog* by Peter Merholz. One in 20 people in the United States claim to have created blogs by 2005.

SISOMOVIES

The DVD format is unleashed in 1997, and rapidly makes itself central to the home entertainment experience. By 2004, consumers in the United States are spending more than $21 billion renting and buying DVDs, and by 2005 the average household owns more than 40 movies on DVD.

KEEP SMILING

The first mobile phone with a camera is manufactured in Japan by Sharp for J-Phone in 2000. Who knew we needed one? Now more camera phones are sold than digital cameras. In the same year, the first full-length feature is produced for distribution on the Internet. Its title: *Quantum Project*.

UNREAL!

Final Fantasy, a movie based on the popular computer game, becomes the first life-like computer-generated feature.

SOME OF THE PEOPLE ALL OF THE TIME

Two years into the new millennium, the total number of television viewers (four years old and up) in China has reached a gigantic 1.115 billion. That's 93.9 percent of the population.

FIRST year that more DVDs are rented than videotapes in the United States is 2003.

HEAR ME!

Eamon's *F**k It. (I Don't Want You Back)* tops the first MEF Official UK Ringtone Charts in June, 2004.

LIVE 8

In a spectacular global sisomo event in June, 2005, Bob Geldof calls to the young people of the world. He asks them to put pressure on the leaders of the world's richest countries to attack the structures of poverty by doubling aid, fully canceling debt, and delivering trade justice to Africa. Geldof tells them, "It is your voice we are after, not your money." The Live 8 concert is a global jukebox created from events in eight cities. In London alone, 12 giant screens are used to cover an area of 472 square meters. The shows are broadcast to 140 countries.

GOOGLE IT

In June, 2005, Google becomes the world's most highly-valued media company, with stock worth $80 billion. Since it was founded in 1998, the search phenomenon has not only grown larger, more profitable and more valuable, it has become more sisomoed. Google Video was also launched in June, so you can search for video and play it in your browser. The ultimate sisomo search engine.

WEB TV

sisomo on the Internet comes of age in the United States. Faster connections are the key, with Nielsen projecting that more than 60 percent of Americans will have high-speed access by the end of 2005. Media companies stampede online and consumers settle back to enjoy the best of sisomo—the engagement of television, the interactivity of online and huge choice and innovation from both.

THE LOOK AND FEEL OF **sisomo...**

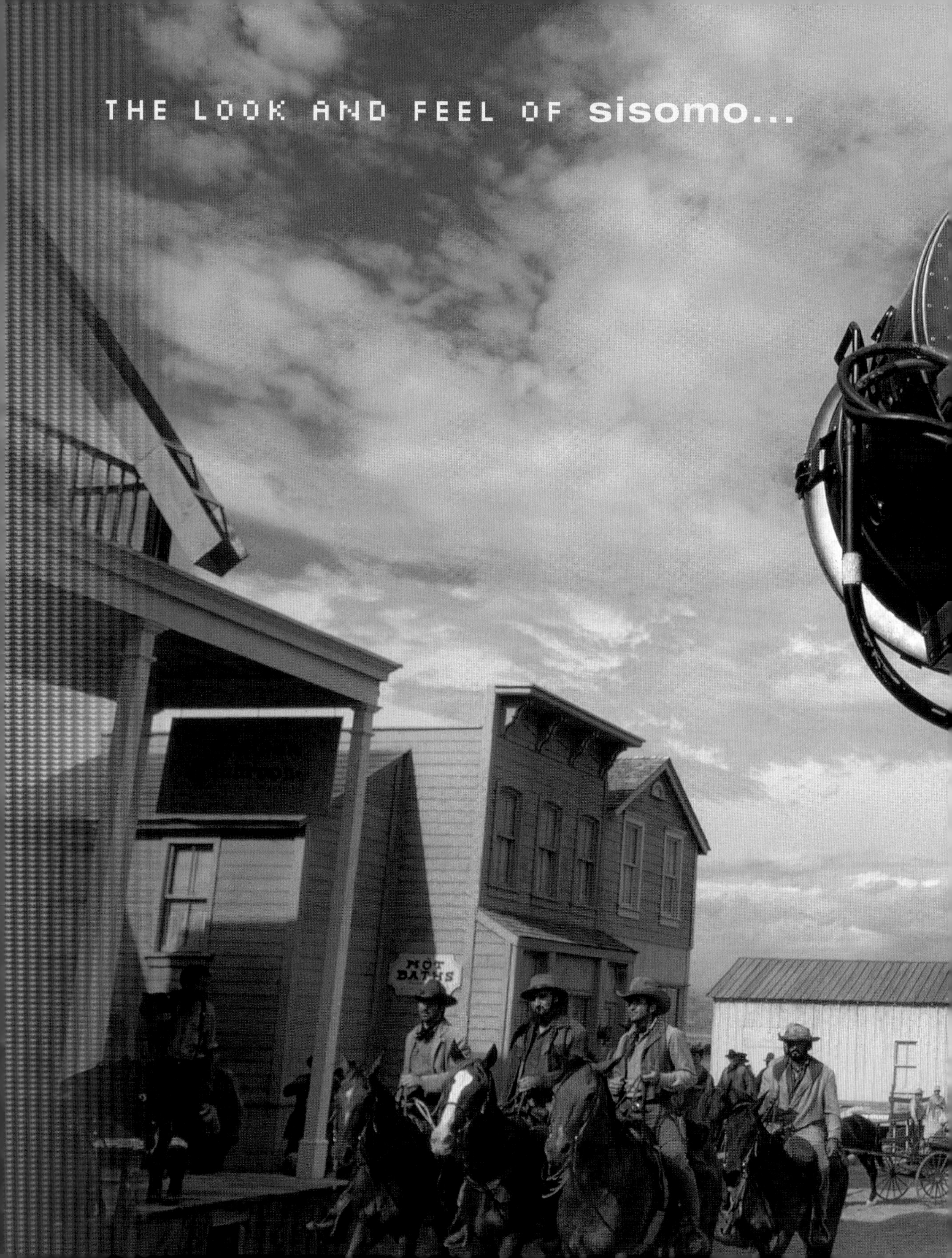

THE EMOTIONAL TUG OF A SOAP OPERA

IN A HANDFUL OF HEARTBEATS.

SLATE 27

TAKE 1

SISOMO—THE FASTEST WAY TO ENGAGE PEOPLE TO THINK WITH THEIR HEARTS AND FEEL WITH THEIR BRAINS.

sisomo
taking the
magic of
storytelling
straight to
the heart.

THE ADRENALINE RUSH OF A GAME

AT YOUR FINGERTIPS

CHAPTER 3

SISOMO ON SCREEN

the big attraction

One of the great stories of the twentieth century was the transformation of everyday life by the dynamic duo of sisomo and screen power.

For millennia, people had experienced Sight, Sound and Motion every day on the streets, at festivals and sports events, out shopping, in markets—but this is not sisomo. Sure, all of them can be entertaining and engaging, but Sight, Sound and Motion need the screen to become the magic of sisomo.

The screen is the child of the twentieth century and sisomo is its most powerful form. sisomo is high-impact emotional content on screen. No screen, no sisomo—it's as simple as that.

When audiences watched the first movies, they were mesmerized by the unique emotional pull of the moving image (and this was Sight and Motion with no Sound!).

Part of the folklore of the movies is the extraordinary impact of these black-and-white images flickering in the darkness. There are well-known stories of audiences panicking as a train rocketed toward them. People ducked for cover—surely it would crush them in its path?

When sound was added to the mix, the temperature only increased. The sisomo experience was always fast, direct and emotional.

The observations of neurologist Donald Calne were central to the story I told in my book, *Lovemarks: the future beyond brands.*

"The essential difference between emotion and reason is that emotion leads to action, while reason leads to conclusions."

It doesn't take a genius to know that emotion is in the driving seat when sisomo goes into action on the screen.

1 THE SCREEN FEELS REAL

At the theater, I often struggle to be convinced by what I see on stage. People come in and out of doors wanting me to believe there is a whole city out there beyond the scenery. It's just too hard. I can't suspend my disbelief.

The screen does something else altogether. Movies, television and games all flow straight into the right side of my brain. Emotional, intuitive, creative.

Men can fly if they wear red and blue costumes? Sure. Cars can crash through brick walls and keep driving? Why not? Characters can cross a city in the blink of an eye? I've seen it happen.

The screen makes real many experiences we could never have in person—and often experiences completely beyond the power of human beings. Multiple views, slow motion, voice-overs, high shots and low shots all pulled together with sound and choreography.

Real events too. The fall of the Berlin Wall in 1989 felt as real in Auckland, New Zealand as it did in Kansas City or Tokyo. Around the globe we saw it happen, as sisomo created

and shaped our minds forever. Even the memories of people actually present were influenced by what they later saw on the screen.

The power of sisomo means that it is now almost inconceivable that any memory can remain the property of just one person. Does Neil Armstrong own the memory of the first step on the moon? Not any more. We were all there with him, inch by historic inch. The things we see on screen become part of our emotional history, part of the world as we picture it in our minds.

As Albert Einstein said, "If I can't picture it, I can't understand it."

2 THE SCREEN FEELS INTIMATE

Sitting in the dark at the movies, sisomo gives us an intimate relationship with those huge faces up on the screen. It is an emotional paradox: the more remote and beautiful they are, the closer we feel to them.

The desire for this experience is now driving the explosive growth of home theater systems, as people seek to indulge themselves, their families and their friends with true sisomo luxury.

The twenty-first century sisomo experience may be a long way from the first television sets, but let's not forget those pioneering boxes. Alive with black-and-white images, they drew families together—and often the neighbors as well. It was, as theorist of the electronic age Marshall McLuhan observed, a true electronic hearth. With few channels to choose from, we all watched the same shows at the same time, creating a special communal intimacy. Just knowing that the family next door and the ones next door to them were all sharing the same experience made us feel closer.

Today television is taking another route to intimacy. Now, with screens in every room and channels created for every personality and interest, the buzz has shifted to the kitchen, with refrigerators sprouting screens and sisomo bubbling alongside the pasta. A recent survey by the National Kitchen & Bath Association shows that the most popular trend in kitchen design is the inclusion of an entertainment area, including a computer and television set.

We love intimacy. We revel in the warmth of feeling special and unique. That's why I can't live without my iPod. I love being able to enrich my life with my very own soundtrack.

Today the desire for intimacy is also unexpectedly transforming the mobile phone. At first restricted to serious business communications and transactions, mobile phone use has blossomed in the past 20 years. sisomo is now turning mobiles into an essential part of our lives, and we keep them close—always. One study says that 60 percent of people leave their phone on while they sleep!

Today we're a long, long way from the simple sound of a phone call. We've gone from flicking through favorite family photographs to sending real-time video images to our friends.

The mobile phone offers us the choices we want, and with sisomo those choices spread in all directions. We can load our special images, customize our ring tone, change it often or make it our signature sound, record what matters to us, watch mini-movies and adorn the handset with cute icons.

THE SCREEN PUMPS OUT CONTENT

People want screens because screens open the door to more stories, more images, more information and more excitement than ever before. The statistics are astounding. Each year the world produces a total of five exabytes of new digital information. According to Roy Williams of the Center for Advanced Computing at the Californian Institute of Technology in Pasadena, this digital torrent is equal to all the words ever spoken by humans. But it is not just the volume that is impressive.

ABCNEWS LIVE COVERAGE
OJ SIMPSON'S CAR

It is the way that, in the form of sisomo, these exabytes can prove so emotionally engaging to audiences around the world. The way they can be transformed on screen from ones and zeroes to images, sounds and action that can thrill, amaze and delight.

That's why in 2004, the most desired electronic gift wasn't an iPod mini or a stereo, it was a plasma television set—the superstar of sisomo. The choice of a plasma was closely followed by a digital camera, a laptop and a regular color television. No surprise to me that every one of these devices has a screen and they have all embraced sisomo.

4 THE SCREEN IS PHYSICAL

Not so long ago, the expression "keep in touch" meant writing a letter or talking on the telephone. Now we can get physical with screens.

A memorable image from Steven Spielberg's *Minority Report* was Tom Cruise as John Anderton searching through files on a transparent screen. As John sifts through information on a 3-D database, his whole body is engaged. He is sisomo personified plucking out a video here, joining it with a conversation there.

The movie *Minority Report* was adapted from a short story by sci-fi genius Philip K. Dick. Strangely, Dick made one of his rare miscalculations when he set his story in 2054. Much of the world of *Minority Report* is already with us. Full-body interfaces are already in the final stages of development.

They will allow complex information to be given the sisomo treatment in applications as varied as traffic control, medical imaging and security. The games industry must be licking its lips in anticipation.

Of course any kid in action on the most primitive touch screen reveals the potential. An instant physical relationship between the body and the screen. True interactivity.

Stores will soon have screens with fantastic-quality soundtracks guiding shoppers on virtual journeys through the store. You will be able to examine produce, dig for background information and visit the countries of origin, all at the touch of a hand. Forget trying to read tiny print on a label. sisomo will be a compelling part of every shopping experience.

I have talked with civic leaders intent on turning their city centers into living museums with the help of touch screen technology. Imagine not only maps that you can touch to get a taste of upcoming events in dramatic sisomo, but also a quick preview tour of a museum you are standing right outside. You grab a painting off the electronic wall and turn it over to view a short movie about the artist. "My kind of place," you decide as you head inside.

I imagine sitting in a plane, feeling my way across the landscape passing beneath the wings. Reaching for unfamiliar towns and cities and exploring them with my fingers on the screen in front of me. I'm sure someone is working on this right now.

THE SCREEN IS A LOYAL COMPANION

Most people still flick on the television set when they get home, "just for company," and around 40 percent of Americans always watch television while eating dinner.

I believe that as more of us choose to live solo lives, our screens will mean even more to us. One in four households in the United States is now a solo household, compared to fewer than one in ten in 1950. That's a lot of people looking to the screen for more company.

Once you get to mobile gadgets, the relationship gets even closer. Mobile phones and PDAs are constant companions for millions always on the move—commuting, shopping, driving the kids. No wonder we're excited about in-vehicle screens for entertainment, not just navigation.

sisomo has transformed the mobile phone from a distant friend who whispers in your ear to a bustling family of images, sounds and action.

On trains in Japan, I have seen young mobile phone fans in action. They swap photographs across the carriage by email, play games and listen to music while scrolling through their image banks. And all on tiny phones they have decorated like shrines with cute charms and tokens: true Lovemarks.

That's why the rule is: never leave home without your keys, your wallet and your mobile phone.

THE SCREEN LOVES TO PLAY

If you're over 40 and don't think video gaming is a critical part of the future, consider these facts:

- Gaming is a $28-billion industry worldwide.
- Around 10 million people worldwide play at least one of the 350 or so massively multiplayer online games (MMOGs) like *EverQuest*.
- Googling *EverQuest* brings up over 3 million results.
- Phone games are accelerating. Sales in 2003 were around $587 million but are projected to grow to $2.6 billion by the end of 2005.
- First-day sales of Microsoft's Xbox game *Halo 2* were $125 million.

"You can't ignore an industry when people queue to buy a game at midnight because they are so desperate to play it ....Nobody queues for music any more."

Gerhard Florin, Electronic Arts

Now put them together. Games have taken sisomo into amazing new directions. Much of their fascination lies in the increasingly rich sisomo experience they offer. As the technology improves, the sisomo potential grows too. The gaming industry is totally in tune with the emotional impact of sisomo, and how we love it!

Movie maker Steven Spielberg predicts a fusion of games and film as games come closer to a storytelling art form. "I think the real indicator will be when someone confesses that they cried at level 17."

More technically, Gerhard Florin of Electronic Arts talks in polygons—the geometric shapes that designers use to make the world of the game look three-dimensional—the key to immersion. He suggests that you cannot express the subtleties of emotion with 5,000 polygons. To do that, you need 30,000 to 50,000 polygons, which is what the new generation of gaming machines offer.

The passions, loyalties and competition among gamers give new life to the expression Loyalty Beyond Reason. Games and their unprecedented sisomo will change many of the ways we interact with the world.

Take education: for all the opposition and finger-wagging, I see games as an important part of education. Imagine generations of kids not just trained on the left side of their brains, but inspired on the right side. Right-side up education.

The cry that games are the end of reading is nonsense. As games become more sophisticated, the significance of what they offer becomes apparent. Writer Steven Johnson points out that one of the walk-throughs (an informal tutorial guide through the game) for *Grand Theft Auto III* is 53,000 words long! That's the length of a decent-sized book.

Unsurprisingly, the American military is investing in games. To address its recruitment challenges, the US Army created a free online game called *America's Army*. Players undertake their first tour of duty alongside fellow soldiers and, without leaving home, experience something of life as a soldier in the army.

The developers claim that the game is played by several million players. According to a survey, the game had between 3,000 and 6,000 players online simultaneously from 2002 until 2005. That's impressive commitment and a great testament to its sisomo delivery.

THE SCREEN IS LIKEABLE

The jury is in. The verdict? People genuinely enjoy their time in front of the screen—and that's probably why we spend so much of it there. Americans spend half their leisure time (and effectively 11 percent of their lives) watching television; Japanese spend even more.

From the early days when people pressed their noses against a storefront to watch the television sets on display to commuters playing games on their laptops and phones, humans have loved the screen.

When a bunch of economists asked the question, "What makes people happy?" they got some surprising results. They asked their subjects to keep a detailed diary of what they were doing and to scale how they were feeling. "We are trying to get a better idea of what people's daily lives are actually like," said Daniel Kahneman of Princeton University.

Dr. Kahneman discovered that the women in the study rated watching television high on the list, ahead of shopping and talking on the phone. (And they ranked taking care of children below cooking and not far above housework!)

The twentieth century had an intense relationship with television. As television itself grows and changes, that intensity is not going to diminish. It's far beyond the sort of relationship we have with our lawn mower or washing machine.

Try googling quotes about lawn mowers and you get a big fat zero. Quotes on television? There are thousands of them. As you will see elsewhere in this book, many are negative, but all are passionate and emotive. Television matters and we feel strongly about it.

THE SCREEN TELLS STORIES

"A picture may be worth a thousand words, but terrific stories are right up there with them." That's what I said in *Lovemarks*. A Lovemark has to have great stories to tell.

Stories help us make sense of our world, to understand the patterns and to make connections. Stories are emotional by nature. They give us perspective and they inspire us to action.

Look at the way the presentation of sports on screen is being shaped by entertainment. And this is happening at the very moment that entertainment feels like tough professional sport.

Sports people today live lives we love to share. Their partners and families, triumphs and failures and the many, many twisting subplots. We even know the back-story of this week's referee!

As journalist Mark Caro points out, much entertainment has become all about competition. Reality TV, for instance, has taken us a long way from quiz shows to *Survivor*, *The Apprentice* and *The Amazing Race*.

It was never a surprise that the best 30-second television commercials created powerful emotional connections like nothing else. They became the most compelling selling tool ever invented because they told stories. Best of all, they told their stories with high-impact sisomo.

The big story of the next decade? The emergence of more and more screens with serious sisomo capabilities.

How about a sponsored soap opera that screens on mobile phones in 60-second episodes? People could catch it during coffee breaks. Or sending personal stories as videos in place of photographs? Camera phones can already capture moving images. Put that together with some smart ideas and sisomo. But why settle for small screens? Beam your stories onto the big screen in the city square. There's already a crowd gathering.

I believe that expertise in creating compelling sisomo stories for the screen will decide who inspires consumers—and who does not.

■ **THE SCREEN IS CONNECTED**
We're a long way from the totem television set in isolated splendor in the living room. Now connections count: screen connected to screen connected to mobile phone, computer and stereo system; whether by snaking cables, wireless or the agile hands and minds of people.

As someone who has struggled to connect all the devices I want, the idea of a home network sounds just great to me. But a word of connection caution. It's the final connection that makes the difference. Connecting to humans is where it counts.

Learn from the sorry story of the remote control. From the Remot-O-Matic and Flashmatic of the 1950s to the Space Command 400, remote controls have been the stuff of comedy. Too complicated to set up, too easy to lose in the cushions, too temperamental.

It wasn't until 1985 that more televisions were sold with remotes than without. Now of course, it's 99 percent, and the number of remotes we juggle is the problem. The average American household is reported to have four remotes. Maybe they lost the other six I still have!

We are promised a media ecosystem in the home, supporting our screens with connections to the Internet, sisomo content via cable and satellite, selection through DVRs and telecommunications. All great technologies, but only technologies.

The sisomo experience will entice people to connected screens, but connected screens alone are no experience at all. The vision of the connected screen will only be made real by a vision for sisomo content.

10 THE SCREEN ADDS UP

People live and/and lives. They like television and their iPod, their computer and the radio and, with all of them, the Internet for broader content and richer entertainment. Most of all, they like to do several things at the same time.

Sixty-four percent of broadband users watch television or read newspapers or magazines at the same time they are online. And if they are wireless broadband users, the figure rises to 71 percent.

Screens no longer stand alone. They must work together to give people the experience they want. The more sisomo a screen experience has, the more attention it will attract.

Why else is video on computers and mobile phones and anywhere else being taken so seriously? sisomo makes a screen experience more valuable, more compelling and more desirable.

11 THE SCREEN SHOWS YOU BELONG

Some of our greatest shared stories have been inspired by sports. Think of the FIFA World Cup or the Olympic Games.

The passion, the grace, the strength, the highs and the moments of shame—this is storytelling at its inspirational peak, infused with drama, intimacy, mystery and the senses all on high alert.

But don't forget: for practically everyone in the world, these mega-events were not firsthand experiences at all.

They came to us via the screen. The intense emotional connection we feel, and return to again and again, is the appeal of classic sisomo. Sight, Sound and Motion create emotional engagement and the strong sense of a shared experience.

On an intimate scale, the same principle will apply. Young people show they belong by talking and texting endlessly, but imagine what will happen as sisomo is added to the mix.

As silent movies were to *The Matrix*, so texting on mobile devices is to the sisomo future. Imagine that wonderful gossipy world of texting enlivened by images and sounds.

I believe that the Age of the Screen is at hand. Sight, Sound and Motion—meet Mystery, Sensuality and Intimacy. Get ready to be inspired!

The Family
of Screens

We love them and watch over them. We lean our family snaps alongside their glassy surfaces and decorate them with our favorite charms. In the evening we are comforted by their friendly glow and in the store are attracted by their tumbling images. In the morning, we search their tiny faces for messages and hang on their every call.

"Individuals' interactions with computers, television and the new media are *fundamentally social and natural*, just like interactions in real life."

Byron Reeves and Clifford Nass,
The Media Equation

Lovemarks are based on a belief that people relate to brands just as they do to one another. sisomo is based on the same principle: people treat screens the way they do other people. If this seems counter-intuitive, blame evolution. Throughout most of our 200,000-year history we have only had social relationships with real live people and objects were always just…objects.

How far from this is your life right now? Count the number of people you have connected with today face-to-face. Now think about the number of connections mediated through phones and email, television and movies.

CHAPTER 4

You are sure you can tell the difference, right? And yet your brain is pretty much the same brain that hunted and gathered and told stories by firelight.

"Modern media now engages old brains."

Byron Reeves and Clifford Nass,
The Media Equation

The truth is, we often don't bother to distinguish between what is physically in front of us and what is mediated. Our emotional responses are the same. That's why we shut our eyes in scary movies and keep repeating: "It's just a movie, it's just a movie." We have to remind logic to kick in and reassure us.

No wonder sisomo has such power. It makes screens more engaging, more compelling and more real.

Let's meet the Family of Screens and check out how they live in the real world. Like all families, they are a fascinating collection of different personalities, ambitions and expertise.

Screen Fun
EXPERIENCE AND ENTERTAINMENT

Television set the pace. It was a welcome and admired visitor to our living rooms from the first day. Sure it was often a love-hate relationship with the tube in the corner, but it was the same relationship we had with teenage children. For all their sullen moments, we loved them for their energy, their fascination with the new and the way they brought life into the house.

If anything changed it was the way our relationships with television became more personal, more intimate. From being the center of attention for the whole family (and the neighbor's kids), television became closer to us as individuals. The remote control sealed the deal, making the relationship truly one-on-one. Sets appeared in bedrooms, kitchens and garages—part friendly human presence, part entertainer, part coach.

When television arrived, it was also billed as an earnest teacher. Trouble was, how much did we really need to know about the sex life of ants? We liked television far too much to turn our living rooms into classrooms.

"We don't want 1,000 channels—we want the one we want to watch."

Nicholas Negroponte, MIT Media Lab

What we really want is something that makes us excited, amazed, thrilled. That's what we demand of all our screens: to be a window into the world of our dreams.

"I want to use television not only to entertain, but to help people lead better lives."

Oprah Winfrey

Television remains such a powerful presence in our lives because it is not a technology but a transformer. A screen that can suck data from DVDs, DVRs, VHS tapes, cameras, the Internet and any other format you care to throw at it, and transform it into exciting and engaging sisomo on screen.

Today television is seducing us anew, with large screens of remarkable quality, deftly coupled to great sound systems. Unbeatable.

Of course, television screens are not content to simply lounge around the house. They find their way to picnics, football games and vacation houses, even joining us on the journey there.

And let's not forget that most entertaining newcomer, the mobile phone. Starting as a small voice in the screen family, it is now commanding attention from all the big players, from games manufacturers to movie makers and online players.

"Phone home!" I don't think so. Have fun on the move and phone home later.

Totem
SCREEN

Lives	In the living room (attached to DVD, DVR, VCR, set-top box, cable, audio system)
Personality	Enjoys being the center of attention
Loves	Big Sights, Big Sounds, Big Motion; Playing to the crowd
Fears	Distractions—people talking on mobile phones or playing games while it's performing; Being trapped in the corner by a nest of cables from all the other hangers-on (DVD, VCR et al.)
Ambition	Being the focus of the family with spectacular events
Favorite song	*Look at Me* —Buddy Holly
sisomo prospects	High

Household
SCREEN

Lives	Anywhere in the house but only connects with network TV
Personality	Unambitious and obedient, happy to be radio with pictures
Loves	Playing one-to-one
Fears	Being rolled by sexier competitors with more sisomo
Ambition	Promotion to Household Screen Plus
Favorite song	*Gotta Serve Somebody* —Bob Dylan
sisomo prospects	Medium

Home Computer Playing Games
SCREEN

Home Theater
SCREEN

Lives	Anywhere in the house, but connects with everyone —network TV, DVD, DVR, game systems
Personality	Open-minded
Loves	The DVD crowd
Fears	Isolation
Ambition	Keeping up with the Technology Joneses
Favorite song	*Raising the Stakes* —Groove Armada
sisomo prospects	High

Lives	In the best room in the house
Personality	Lives to show off to groups— the bigger the better
Loves	Even Bigger Sight, Bigger Sound, Bigger Motion; Being loved by all the family, and lusted after by their friends; Taking part in special events, sports, firsts, award shows
Fears	Cheap sound equipment
Ambition	Domination
Favorite song	*I Love How You Love Me* —Bobby Vinton
sisomo prospects	Very High

Mobile Phone
SCREEN

Lives	Always by your side
Personality	Sociable
Loves	Add-ons—camera, music, flash-light, mirror, video clips; The life of an entertainer
Fears	Being "just a phone"
Ambition	To be indispensable
Favorite song	*I Get Around* —The Beach Boys
sisomo prospects	Very High

Movie Theater
SCREEN

Lives	In multiplexes
Personality	Big show-off
Loves	Having "Biggest Sight, Biggest Sound, Biggest Motion" tattooed on its chest; Attention—but today has to work much harder for it; The "-er" words—louder, bigger, faster
Fears	Home theater
Ambition	Irresistible spectacle at least once a week
Favorite song	*Harder, Better, Faster, Stronger* —Daft Punk
sisomo prospects	High

Portable DVD
SCREEN

Lives	Out and about
Personality	A real loner
Loves	Getting up-close and personal
Fears	Other screens (we call it screen-envy)
Ambition	To get past fad status
Favorite song	*Travelin' Man* —Bob Seger
sisomo prospects	Medium

Music Player
SCREEN

Lives	Within earshot
Personality	Cool dude, but tends to be introspective
Loves	Intimacy
Fears	Too much competition from mobile phones
Ambition	To team up with video
Favorite song	*I Put a Spell on You* —Van Morrison
sisomo prospects	Very High

Game Systems—Xbox, PlayStation, Game Boy

SCREEN

Screen Players
GAME FOR ANYTHING

The Japanese call them *oya yubi sedai*—the thumb generation. Millions of young people who can type with their thumbs almost as fast as anyone else can speak.

These are the thumbs that have been trained on Game Boys and PlayStations. They are itching to touch screens, wind-up video on mobile phones and dive even deeper into the world of games.

For this generation, anything with a screen that lets them join the game is a friend for life. Television, mobile phones, building façades, anything.

Even the smallest screens know they can excel in the brightly-colored world of the old chase-and-eat-'em challenges. Small screens that are working out at the digital gym and have achieved perfect definition!

Will game screens capture older players? And will young players welcome product placement, competitions and viral advertising into their world? Stick around and see which way the thumb points.

Lives	Any place, any time
Personality	Party animal
Loves	Playing new games, especially online
Fears	Getting stuck with SCREENYBOPPERS; Too much product placement
Ambition	All the world a player
Favorite song	*Born to Be Wild* —Steppenwolf
sisomo prospects	Very High

the future on screen 57

Mobile
Phone
SCREEN

Lives	In pockets and bags, on belts
Personality	Gregarious thumb buddy
Loves	Being in touch; Playing cool games; Learning new tricks
Fears	Getting fat and heavy and being left behind
Ambition	World domination
Favorite song	*You Ain't Seen Nothin' Yet* —Bachman Turner Overdrive
sisomo prospects	Very High

Computer
at Home
SCREEN

Lives	Where people play
Personality	Game for anything
Loves	Attracting more fans with new tricks; Being sociable if given the chance
Fears	Windows (just kidding)
Ambition	More sisomo
Favorite song	*My World Is Empty Without You* —The Supremes
sisomo prospects	Very High

In-Store Players
SHAPE-SHIFTERS

The Family of Screens likes to be seen where it counts, and this family knows that one place it does count is in-store. Do screens like shopping? You bet. They're all over it, turning shoppers into buyers:

- Screens that love to display themselves. Uninhibited exhibitionists that know their sisomo makes the shopping experience more stimulating and more fun.

- Screens that are members of specialty retail television networks with a new commitment to delighting and engaging consumers. Their track record isn't great, and they are determined to catch up.

- Screens that shape-shift at will. "Any size, any shape, any way up" is the in-store screen motto. Want to see out the window of a display bus? Here's a screen to show you the world. Need a stunning backdrop to a fashion show in-store? Enter the super-size screen with matching accessories.

- Screens that are a soft touch. Put a finger on them and they burst out sisomo all over. Picturesque vineyards on rolling hillsides with the wine racks, personality chefs with their favorite recipes alongside the produce, simple color- and shape-matching in the baby care aisle.

Lives	In malls, stores, window displays
Personality	Eager beaver
Loves	To capture attention and entertain
Fears	Being over-exposed and capturing no one's attention; Being used as wallpaper
Ambition	To turn shoppers into buyers
Favorite song	*Hear My Train A Comin'* —Jimi Hendrix
sisomo prospects	High

Billboard
SCREEN

Screenery
THE PASSING PARADE

Mega-screens like the outdoor life. They are never happier than hanging around tall buildings sending big messages to the tiny people way down in the street below. They love surprising the thousands who pour across the crossings outside Shinjuku Station in Tokyo or gape at sisomo in Times Square, New York.

The big outdoor screens have taken sisomo experiences to a new level and they are not done yet. They are traveling the world, taking their larger-than-life sisomo with them.

These are screens that like to surprise. Watch for them riding on the sides of trucks, sitting up on billboards and making guest appearances at rock concerts.

These screens are crazy about events—and events are crazy about them. Giant screens have become an essential part of the sports stadium experience. They thrill the crowds with their sweeping close-ups and slow-mo reveals. These screens respond to the roar of the crowd.

They're sisomonumental!

Lives	In the great outdoors
Personality	Inferiority complex—thinks bigger and brighter is better
Loves	To seize attention
Fears	Blending in with the crowd
Ambition	To come up with endless breakthrough ideas
Favorite song	*Action in the Streets*—Bruce Springsteen
sisomo prospects	High

Travelin' Screen
ON THE ROAD AGAIN

These screens have itchy feet. They're always ready to put out a thumb to hitch a ride in anything that will let them settle back and entertain the troops.

You'll find these screens in the back of airplane seats showing movies and other sisomo to cheer up the people traveling with them. They are also to be found in cars and trucks, even if they do have to take a back seat. They like to team up with DVDs so they can give their passengers good sisomo as the countryside flies by the window. Sixteen percent of American consumers reportedly have a DVD player in their car.

Sure, sometimes they get a little irritated by the mobile screens with their games and music and the Game Boys drive them mad. Still, even on the move, they're coming to an arrangement with the gaming passengers and the online crowd.

But traveling screens are not always on the go. They also know when to stop for a night's good entertainment in a comfortable hotel. It's nice to put their feet up and get together with the DVDs, videos, and Internet for the evening.

Lives	At 30,000 feet
Personality	Desperate
Loves	Any attention it can get
Fears	Being superseded by portable devices with more sisomo
Ambition	To become a personal companion
Favorite song	*Devoted To You* —Everly Brothers
sisomo prospects	High

In-Auto SCREEN

Lives	In the backseat (hopefully)
Personality	Distracted
Loves	Letting the kids get away with murder; To be in the front seat, where it promises to behave
Fears	Playing second fiddle to the view out the window
Ambition	To become a personal companion
Favorite song	*Can't Take My Eyes Off You* —Frankie Valli and The Four Seasons
sisomo prospects	Medium

In-Room Hotel SCREEN

Lives	In every hotel and motel
Personality	A loner who wants to be liked but hasn't yet got the personality for it
Loves	Personal attention; Getting busy with check-out; Useful information
Fears	Competition from personal screens, laptops, portable DVD players and even mobile phones
Ambition	To become a personal companion
Favorite song	*Let's Spend The Night Together* —The Rolling Stones
sisomo prospects	Medium

Computer at work
SCREEN

Screen Workers
ON THE SERIOUS SIDE OF THE STREET

Hard work never hurt anyone and you won't get a computer screen to complain that it's on too long and stared at too hard, day after day.

These are the workhorse screens that double as entertainers when the time is right. They'd love to have rich floods of sisomo surging through their cables. But there's always work to be done. Now if only work could become a little more fun!

Remember these members of the screen family when they are hard at work creating sisomo for others in the screen family.

Lives	In the office
Personality	Dutiful but loves to break out and party
Loves	Being sociable (given the chance)
Fears	Being too entertaining
Ambition	To motivate change
Favorite song	*Work For Love* —Ministry
sisomo prospects	Medium to High

Power Point
SCREEN

Computer at home
SCREEN

Lives	For meetings!
Personality	Bossy
Loves	Making a difference with a bit of sisomojo
Fears	More bad press; Being blamed for destroying corporate intellectual life
Ambition	To motivate change
Favorite song	*Nice to Be With You* —The Gallery
sisomo prospects	Very High

Lives	On a desk
Personality	Entertaining know-it-all
Loves	Being distracted from the task at hand; Keeping in touch; Entertainment and shopping
Fears	Being taken too seriously
Ambition	To strike a life/work balance
Favorite song	*Getting Better* —The Beatles
sisomo prospects	Very, Very High

PDA
SCREEN

22

7.30am

Lives	Wherever it's needed
Personality	Nerdy kid who needs to get a life
Loves	Knowing everything
Fears	Being dismissed as an address book
Ambition	To live with the phone family
Favorite song	*From Small Things (Big Things One Day Come)* —Bruce Springsteen
sisomo prospects	Medium

Screen Exchange
TRANSACTION ACTION

Not too much sisomo action with these guys. They'd like to be more entertaining but they are so useful that no one seems to notice how much more they are capable of.

Transactions are essential—but once you make them fast, accurate, and efficient, where else is there to go? These guys are focused on transactions when they should be out there forming relationships with consumers.

Some of them do make an effort. A few kiosk screens try to make a connection with consumers, but it's still functional—not emotional—with sisomo a distant murmur.

With mobile phones learning how to make transactions along with everything else, watch out. Transactions will be wrapped up in a sisomo package rather than be left fending for themselves.

Computer at home
SCREEN

ATM
SCREEN

Lives	On a desk
Personality	Hard worker with an eye for a bargain
Loves	Buying stuff; Bringing the world into the home; eBay.com and Amazon.com
Fears	Getting too slow; Information overload
Ambition	To be indispensable
Favorite song	*Taking Control* —Aphex Twin
sisomo prospects	Very, Very High

Lives	On walls all around town
Personality	Nothing anyone can remember
Loves	Getting it right
Fears	Emotional commitment
Ambition	To have more fun
Favorite song	*Money, Money, Money* —Abba
sisomo prospects	Low

Kiosk
SCREEN

Home Appliance
SCREEN

Lives	Wherever it's needed
Personality	Closet entertainer
Loves	To be right at hand with whatever you desire
Fears	Wasting time (can be a little abrupt)
Ambition	To have more fun
Favorite song	*We've Only Just Begun* —The Carpenters
sisomo prospects	Very High

Lives	At home
Personality	Narrow-minded
Loves	Keeping to the job at hand
Fears	People who can't follow simple instructions
Ambition	To make tasks easier and more fun
Favorite song	*You Make It Easy* —Air
sisomo prospects	High

Commercial Security
SCREEN

Screen Watch
HERE'S LOOKING AT YOU

These screens are too busy keeping track of everyone else to do much sisomo work themselves. Secretive and dogmatic, they are respected rather than loved. Part of their problem is that while they have the sight and motion thing worked out, everything has to be done on the quiet. That's security for you.

Recently some of the Security Family have teamed up with directional sound tools to offer the full sisomo package. And we're not just talking spy work here. Parents wanting to keep track of their kids, households needing to check out visitors at the door. Not exactly the full emotional sisomo package, but it's a start.

Worth keeping an eye on.

Lives	For the moment
Personality	Secretive
Loves	Not being noticed
Fears	Changes to routine
Ambition	No mistakes
Favorite song	*God Is In The House* —Nick Cave and the Bad Seeds
sisomo prospects	Low

Home Security
SCREEN

Lives — On guard

Personality — Trustworthy

Loves — The job 24/7

Fears — Power cuts

Ambition — No mistakes

Favorite song — *Watching You Watching Me*
—Jethro Tull

sisomo prospects — Low

Family Ties
GETTING TOGETHER

The really big story about the Family of Screens is how they are getting together. This is a family that didn't talk to each other for years. Now new conversations and opportunities are bringing them closer and it's getting tough to tell who's who.

As writer Kendall Hailey said, "The great gift of family life is to be intimately acquainted with people you might never even introduce yourself to, had life not done it for you." It's the same with the Family of Screens.

The family that plays together stays together. That's how it will be with the Family of Screens. Without sisomo, the Family of Screens is trapped in adolescence: self-obsessed and fascinated by technology. With sisomo, the family can mature and connect emotionally—with ideas, imagination and inspirations everywhere.

Watch as family members dig into fantastic new sisomo opportunities.

Computer screens are showing the sisomo flair that once only television dared express. And television is reaching out and starting to love sisomo direct from the Internet. Let's not forget mobile phones. Once happy to keep to themselves, they have jumped right into the center of the sisomo world of movie clips, short family videos and music.

So this family's toast is "To sisomo!" The powerful content that makes screens come alive.

5 Notice what is static (like the boring office memo you just sent) and think how it could be sisomoed.

4 Rent or buy three great movies on DVD. Check out how sisomo delivers emotional content and take it to heart.

3 Touch every screen you see and see if it reacts. You might be surprised!

2 Talk to young people about how they use their mobile devices. Better still, listen to them!

1 Sign up for a video production, filmmaking or animation class. Learn new skills that you can use in a sisomo world.

CHAPTER 5

A sampling of my favorite sisomo experiences

sisomo

IN ACTION

RED BULL AIR RACE

The Red Bull Air Race World Series is red-hot excitement for the pilots who fly in it and a compelling experience for visitors to www.redbullairrace.com. Injected with sisomo to the power of the fourth dimension,

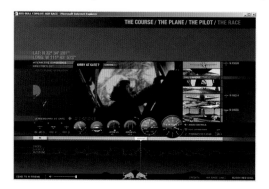

Red Bull has created a site that puts you in the cockpit or—if you prefer—hanging off the front wheels of these specialty aircraft. The roar of the engines, the giddy aerobatics and the spectacular views all spell sisomo.

LORD OF THE RINGS

My home is on the edge of the world in New Zealand—and that's where movie

director Peter Jackson creates his sisomo spectaculars. Bringing home 11 Academy Awards, including Best Director, for his epic *Lord of the Rings: The Return of the King*, Jackson was born to be a sisomo magician. Combining convincing computer-generated action with natural scenery and actors, he turbo-charges his movies with a sisomo essential: great storytelling. Jackson demonstrates the ability to create great sisomo anywhere in the world. sisomo yields to no boundaries; it recognizes no borders.

SKY CHURCH

The sisomo experience can be as intimate as a video sent to your mobile phone or your favorite sportsperson tall as a tree on a stadium replay screen. For sisomo, small is beautiful, and so is gigantic. That's why I am a champion of sisomo; it's not scale that makes the difference, but the emotional burst. You can find both a big screen and

a compelling emotional experience at the Frank Gehry–designed Experience Music Project in Seattle. Celebrating the past, present and future, this music museum boasts the Sky Church, a huge space with a cathedral ceiling and one of the largest video screens in the world. What do you get on a 40 by 70 foot screen? Major sisomojo! This screen pours out a kaleidoscope of images to the sound of great music from an amazing 50-speaker sound system. On top of the mega-screen, another 18 screens roll montages of key rock 'n' roll moments. sisomo rocks!

24

Anyone who has seen Fox TV's drama 24 has experienced sisomo on adrenaline. The compulsive story of a 24-hour crisis played out in real time. Each hour of 24

is an exhausting race against time, as hero Jack Bauer struggles to avoid disaster on an epic scale. The 24 mobile series is something else again. A series of 60-second episodes based on the original show and produced for mobile phones—mobisodes, of course. Fox does the story, Vodafone the distribution and sisomo the experience. I've caught up with movie previews on my phone, but 24 in 60 seconds? Let me at it.

THE SOPRANOS

My favorite sisomo on television? *The Sopranos*. From Alabama 3's unmistakable theme music to the closing vignette, this show is the perfect expression of grown-up sisomo. sisomo can be subtle and sophisticated, as well as provocative and energetic. For me *The Sopranos* draws sisomo up close to Lovemarks: complex stories that

twist, turn and surprise, true psychological resonance, a wonderful array of personalities, an astonishing mix of emotions in every episode, from joy to disgust and back again, and the most evocative opening credits ever. Are all television shows sisomo? If they have Sight, Sound and Motion they certainly are. Are all television shows masterpieces? No, they are not. Doing great sisomo is an art as well as a science.

THE TALBY MOBILE BY MARC NEWSON

The great thing about sisomo's life on screen is that screens are getting cooler by the day. Designers have been quick to see that the home of something as compelling as sisomo is a place they want to hang their hats. Top of the list for me is Australian designer Marc Newson.

To call Marc a designer is like calling Bob Dylan a guitar player. He has designed some of the most beautiful objects I have ever seen, and the top of the list has got to be his mobile phone for Talby. Sleek, mysterious and sensual, it feels like sisomo heaven. I watched some young Japanese playing network games on these magical Newson phones. It was like being sucked into the sisomo future.

Says Marc Newson: "I think about the future all the time, in terms of how what I do will exist in the future. I try to visualize the world in ten years and imagine how this thing I am designing now will be perceived."

TIMES SQUARE

When I want to immerse myself in sisomo I walk uptown from my home in TriBeCa to Times Square, the only neighborhood in New York where it is actually illegal for a sign not to be illuminated. This is an experience that just gets better. Forty million annual visitors can't be wrong. Times Square has become a laboratory for every fad and fashion you can think of. Want to design your own Nike shoe? Do it right here via your mobile phone. Want to watch other people partying? Check out the two-day launch of the CK One fragrance held in a three-story perfume bottle. That's Times Square for you: financial institutions

and fashion houses rub shoulders with the NASDAQ and the US Armed Forces' recruitment drive. The atmosphere is electric. Literally. My bet is that as the cost of space increases, sound will feature on more screens. Directional sound has become very sophisticated in retail, in museums, in theme parks. I look forward to strolling around Times Square or Tokyo's Shibuya or along the Bund in Shanghai, with screen-sounds in my wake. sisomotion indeed.

SISOMO SPORTS

I sometimes think the two "s's" in sisomo stand for sport. Is there any other activity that brings so much drama and color to the sisomo experience? The Olympics, the World Cup and hundreds of other events light up our screens with action, energy and the roar of the crowd. On the day of a

big rugby game in New Zealand, we can have half a dozen different sisomo experiences. Start with a series of spine-tingling ads for the game on television. Then check out the form in past games on a portable DVD player with a beer in the yard. Listen for the chant of the All Blacks' Maori haka as someone plays adidas *Beatrugby* online. Then there are big screens at the local sports bar with sisomo action whipping up the fans. At the game, the giant screens pulse with inspirational visuals and, of course, the critical replays. Is there sound in that giant-screen sisomo? Who can hear for the roar of the crowd?

FABLE

Games like *Doom* and *Quake* are packed with sisomo. Engaging, heart-stopping and totally immersive. But there are other, more intimate, games that bring sisomo to our computers, laptops and television screens as well. One that appeals to me for infusing the Lovemarks qualities of Mystery, Sensuality

and Intimacy with sisomo is *Fable*. This role-playing game from Peter Molyneux for the Xbox allows you to create your life story from childhood through adulthood and on to old age. As you play, you face opportunities and challenges, make friends and allies, shape your own appearance, skills and reputation. This is a world where what you do matters. The game asks: "Will you travel the road of the righteous or lead a life of evil? Play the *Fable* game to discover your destiny!" And it all begins with a storybook, the traditional words, "once upon a time..." and sisomo.

U2: ZOO TV

Pink Floyd may have been in the first wave to start the sisomo revolution at rock concerts, but for me it was U2 who gave the definitive sisomo performance on stage. Go back in

time to 1992. You are at the fantastic Zoo TV concert, over-awed by giant video screens, by the stage crowded with monitors and even by video signage that gives breaking news as you wait for the band to begin. When U2 gets on stage, the sisomo action is extreme. Bono grabs a camera and videos himself. Giant Bono images loom on the screens surrounding the band. He gives the camera to people in the audience to create their own sisomo action on screen. Once you lock that sight and motion with the U2 sound you have an emotional mix that can bond thousands into a single soul. The most moving moment? When you see Dr. Martin Luther King speaking as U2 plays *In the Name of Love*. Irresistible. That's why, when Apple was looking for the perfect musicians to be associated with their first colorful iPod, they chose U2.

MACROMEDIA FLASH

I'm no software guru, but I know the site I started with New Zealander Brian Sweeney, www.nzedge.com, has been sisomoed, and that it was thanks to Macromedia Flash software. Maybe our next step will be to get into Animutation—a way of using Flash to create animated videos. Animutation is sisomo to go. First used by 13-year-old Neil Cicierega from Massachusetts, Animutation is fun and crazy and the ideal DIY tool.

Hundreds of Flash artists, musicians and fans are making animutations to take more sisomo online. The style is often raw, the ideas irreverent and the images random, but the effect is electric. Want to check it out? Try www.albinoblacksheep.com/flash/animutation/. One of my favorites is Elvis Lives in Flash by Sners, with its dancing bananas and cool digitized film clips.

THE HIRE

If anyone doubted the power of sisomo, those doubts would have been blasted away by the amazing mini-movies made for BMW in 2001. As the advertising world anguished over the demise of the 30-second television commercial, BMW went for a bigger idea in a different medium. sisomo on the Internet. David Fincher, director of *Seven* and *Fight Club*, was the perfect producer. As a key

crossover director from advertising into movie making, Fincher's mastery of sisomo took new creative ground online. The first series of five movies presented *The Hire*, with Clive Owen driving a series of BMWs. There aren't plots so much as situations—action, car chases, bad behavior, famous faces. Are these advertisements, product placements, art or sponsored events? It no longer matters. What does matter is superb sisomo resonating online.

VLOGS

Once blogging took off, it wasn't long before bloggers started to eye up sisomo. Enter the vlog, a blog that loves video. Today vlogs are only a small outbreak of sisomo, but watch them grow like a weed. Why? Because

they put passionate, knowledgeable and committed people in charge. Sometimes they are banal, often they are crude, obsessive or downright weird, but they feel to me like the beginnings of the movies. People capturing the life around them with energy and enthusiasm. I like *Rocketboom*, created by Andrew Baron and fronted by Amanda Congdon. From Monday through Friday, this show offers three minutes of news, opinion and insight. Amanda is the sisomo VJ, orchestrating an ambitious repertoire of sisomo on screen. At the end of Amanda's three minutes, you really feel connected with her view of the world. Isn't that what news is supposed to do?

"When I auditioned, I went, 'So, you're gonna take me and put it online? Cool!'" says Amanda Congdon. "I never really understood what I was getting into, that it would be so much more than that."

MUSIC VIDEOS
To anyone under 30, the spirit of sisomo is the music video. In the 1980s, the launch of a new video by a major star was a big deal.

These intense bursts of creativity shaped new forms of storytelling and on-screen visualization as well as fashion, beauty, dance, culture, advertising and, yes, music. This was always sisomotion at a hundred miles an hour. Dominated by MTV for two decades, the music video is finding a new life on different screens—computers, mobile phones, game systems, portable music players.

Dave Goldberg, of Yahoo! Music, says: "Not counting porn, music video is clearly the most popular video content online."

BEST BUY ESCAPE STORES
sisomo was born to make emotional connections with shoppers in-store. Retail TV networks (Wal-Mart, Tesco, Ralph's), interactive screens and pure-experience screens will be joined by screens carried by shoppers—the mobile phone. This future is already being invented in Best Buy's Chicago Escape concept store. Created for the gadget-hungry among us, the idea is to tap into the passions of technology enthusiasts to see what turns them on. Not only are all the cutting-edge screens from phones to games to computers to cameras on display, you can give them a test drive. You can also hire big screen home theater setups to give some sisomo clout to your next party. With catering. This is R&D that shoppers can participate in.

HANNSPREE
I still find myself loving one of the senior sisomo experiences: relaxing on a comfortable couch in front of a big television screen with great sound. Now, thanks to Hannspree, a smart Taiwanese company, the television set doesn't have to be square. I'm not talking content for once, I mean shape. Hannspree is developing themed television sets in all kinds of shapes, sizes and appearances. Show off your passions

with your choice of television. My favorite takes a basketball shape complete with stitching lines—but there is also the baseball set, the Mickey Mouse set and the stylish Hannsvaas set, shaped rather mysteriously as a cello. OK, it might be a fad—but it adds fun to the sisomo experience. Explore your personality at www.hannspree.com.

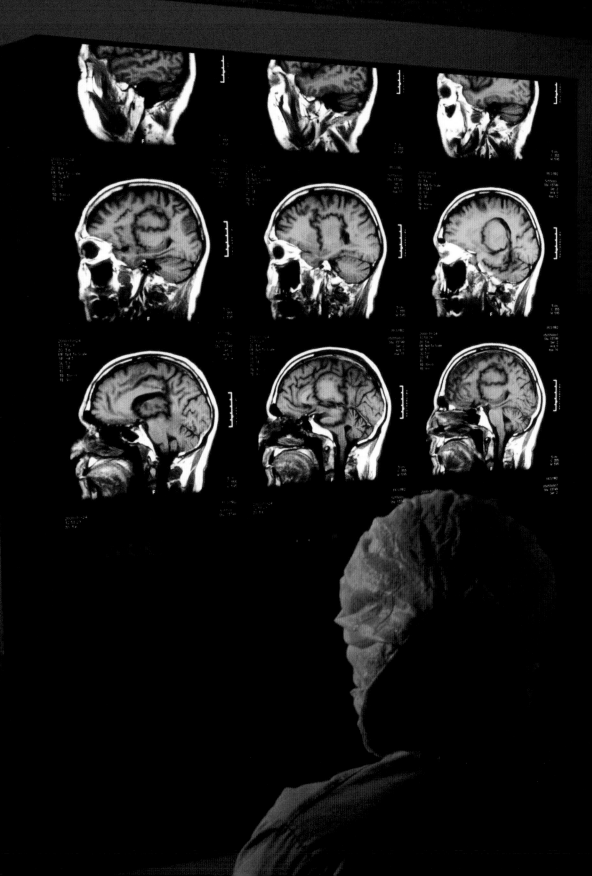

A quick quiz for the

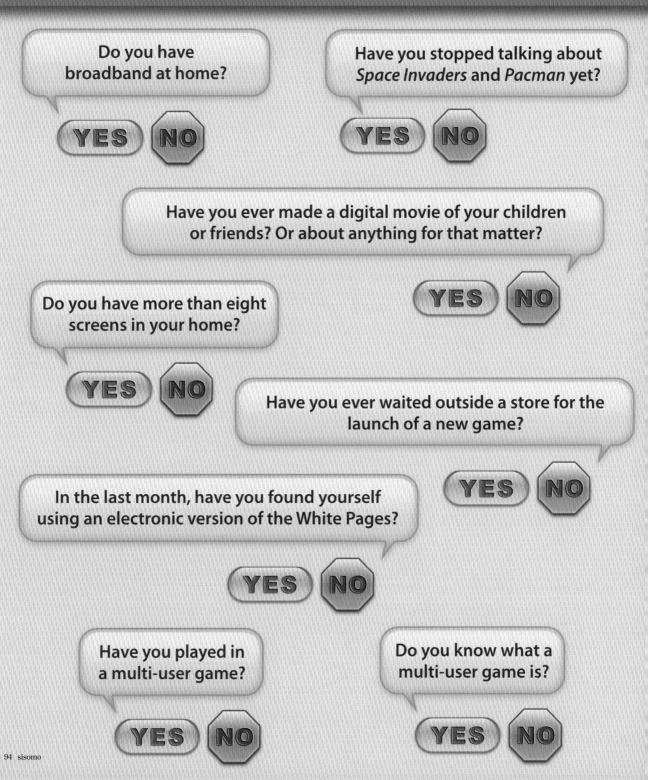

Have you emailed photos from your mobile phone? OK, how about music? Anything?

YES **NO**

Do you watch at least five movies a month?

YES **NO**

Does the thought of watching a video on your mobile phone make your heart beat faster?

YES **NO**

Have you ever joined the crowd at a sports bar to watch a big game?

YES **NO**

Is your television screen bigger than your dining room table?

YES **NO**

Do you own more than 50 DVDs?

YES **NO**

10: yes—you're sisomotivated. Less than 5: find a comfortable chair and read a book.

FIVE THINGS TO DO TOMORROW

5 Check your screen-based communications for Sight, Sound and Motion. Make sure all of your brand icons and characters can move on screen.

4 Imagine the Sight, Sound and Motion of your product or brand—how do you work sisomo in?

3 Shop for a video game. Ask for something action-packed and cinematic. Play it and experience the future of sisomo entertainment.

2 Whenever you see a billboard or a sign, imagine a screen instead.

1 Take some pictures of your everyday life. Start a photo-blog and share them with the world. Better yet, start a video-blog.

CHAPTER 6

WHERE DOES THIS LEAVE TELEVISION?

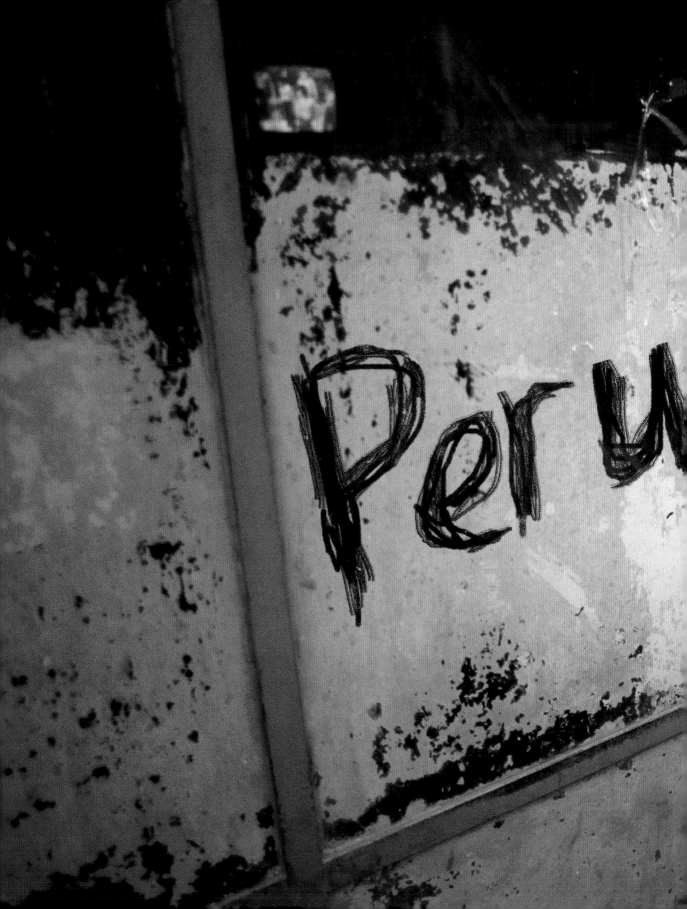

Since the 1980s, television has grown fast in emerging nations. Now over 2.5 billion people in these countries are estimated to have regular access. What does television offer them? Like the places, it varies hugely. Often a wave of Western-style programs—news, movies, soaps, children's shows, music and sports—is followed by local versions or genuinely local programs. Like everywhere else, the effects of television are hugely diverse. It can raise expectations and build new confidence, educate and inform, provoke and entertain.

ABOUT TELEVISION

1

"TV is dead."

Don't count on it. The television screen remains the most powerful way to connect emotionally with consumers—nothing else comes close. That's why advertisers entertain other options but remain committed. Television is still the biggest advertising medium by far.

sisomo is breathing new life into the television experience through the wonder of digital technology. People don't just want the big screen—they want the full sisomo package. In 2000, 21 percent of households in the United States owned a home theater system. In January 2005, 33 percent did. Digital television brings new quality and rich sound and scale to the picture, as well as the beginnings of true interactivity. And the promise of 3-D television—without the glasses.

And at the same time, television content is transforming with extra sisomo. Reality shows that tap into the roots of human behavior. Who's in, who's out and who'll win?

Sports play in the same territory and now give viewers the tools to be well-informed commentators—as well as opinionated ones—with a flood of performance statistics and computer visualizations. Understand the strategic skill in formerly elitist events like the America's Cup; track never-before-seen views from cameras everywhere—in helmets, in skis, in the ball itself. Then there's the news, which is now a speedy mix of entertainment, information and personality rapidly heading in a very different direction from its print ancestors.

Television is proving to be open-hearted. Media companies battle over broadcast versus cable versus satellite versus the Internet, and everyone versus mobile phones, but the people watching don't care as long as it has enough sisomo to capture their imaginations.

TV hasn't died; it is living the spirit of sisomo.

2

"No one watches television any more."

There is no doubt about it. Network television no longer holds undisputed sway over people's entertainment options in the United States. And that's got to be a good thing. The pattern is the same in other developed markets.

In the 1960s, advertisers could reach 80 percent of American women by airing a spot simultaneously on the three networks. Today people have far more choice and far more control, and they like it this way.

People work late and their kids have demanding schedules. In the United States, people are out of their homes 65 percent more of the time than they were two decades ago. Nearly 20 percent of adults aged between 25 and 54 are not back home before nine or ten in the evening.

And yet, despite the pressure on their time, people watch a lot of television. According to a US Government study, people spend roughly half their free time watching television, although the actual hours vary according to education and other factors. Young people are consistently enthusiastic. They spend an average of three hours a day—or nearly four hours when you include DVDs and pre-recorded shows—watching the television screen. Two-thirds have a television set in their bedroom and around half of them live in homes where the television is left on most of the time.

But television is not simply the backdrop to everyday life. It continues to offer the largest shared experiences we can take part in. Sports are the most obvious example. The FIFA World Cup final attracted a global audience of 1.1 billion viewers. And an incredible 4.2 million Koreans took to the streets to watch their victory over Italy televised on big screens.

Television remains an integral part of our sisomo lives.

3

"DVRs will kill television advertising."

We all know a lot about television, so let's start with DVRs. First there's the acronym. Never a good sign. Digital Video Recorder. Who needs to know so much about a box with buttons? DVRs have to get past the technology and connect with people.

It's been proven over and over. People will move to adopt once an innovation is easy to use and priced right, irreplaceable and irresistible. The iPod, the mobile phone, the digital camera. People love them all. The uptake of the DVR has not been stellar so far because it fails the basic test: it's not easy to use or priced right, it's not indispensable and it's certainly not yet irresistible.

DVRs add cost and complexity, but most of all they demand attention. Attention to making the right choice. Attention to keeping up. Attention so you don't miss out. We know that people are time-poor and that attention is just what they are short of.

The beauty of television is its simplicity: no analysis, no tough decisions, and always the potential of something new and exciting. You don't have to manage television, you experience it.

DVRs make television a very different option in a busy life. Fans of the DVR way of life so far tend to be organized and focused. They know what they want—and what they don't. The flow of television is not for them.

Where does this put television advertising? If anything kills television advertising it will be television advertising. The same commercials locked in the same format played over and over. Being boring puts consumers off. Mix in sisomo and television's appeal is enduring.

4

"In-store television is boring."

Ain't that the truth. The technology infrastructure is way ahead of how it's being used.

It's not a new idea to have television in-store—and maybe that's the problem. Pipe it in, put it on and pump it out. No wonder store screens feel like wallpaper. Shoppers have become desensitized. *Act* boring for long enough, and people will assume you *are* boring. Terms like "Captive Audience Network" just nail it.

Debates over broadcast TV and narrowcast TV become irrelevant when you behave like outcast TV.

The potential of television in-store is only beginning to be tapped. Wal-Mart TV reaches 130 million viewers every four weeks, making it the fifth-largest television network in the United States. Imagine the possibilities of a more entertaining, more informative and more engaging experience for shoppers and retailers, and the greater ability to reach the right shoppers when it matters for advertisers.

One study has scoped out some possibilities for the medium. Imagine the impact of sisomo on these findings. Most people felt TV in-store increased their shopping pleasure—and they chose to stay longer and spend more. The younger they were, the more they liked it. A lively content mix helped to win attention and increase engagement. Interesting and relevant product information as well as community news. As always, music mattered. The principle is simple: let empathy guide you. Shoppers want to be relaxed rather than energized. As to effectiveness, the metrics were impressive—with sales increasing an estimated 1.5 percent.

Screens in-store are a fantastic opportunity to create inspiring, provocative sisomo experiences that shoppers love. And watch out for another possibility. From screens on shelves to screens on shoppers. Yes, the mobile phone again. The screen that allows her to compare prices, check ingredients and pay before she gets to the checkout. With sisomo, the shopping experience can be transformed at every point.

5

"Everyone hates television."

People have always loved talking about how much they hate television.

"I find television very educating. Every time somebody turns on the set, I go into the other room and read a book."

Groucho Marx

"Television is chewing gum for the eyes."

Frank Lloyd Wright

"I wish there were a knob on the TV to turn up the intelligence. There's a knob called 'brightness,' but that doesn't work."

Anonymous

"I hate television. I hate it as much as peanuts. But I can't stop eating peanuts."

Orson Welles

"Television is an invention that permits you to be entertained in your living room by people you wouldn't have in your home."

David Frost

"The smallest bookstore still contains more ideas of worth than have been presented in the entire history of television."

Andrew Ross

All this wit and passion only clinches the argument: television is the most powerful, popular entertainment source in the world. People care about it. People react to it. And—even though no one will admit to it—people watch it.

6

"The 30-second ad is dead in the water."

The 30-second spot has been the standard of television advertising since the 1970s. The rationale? Consistent blocks of time make scheduling easier, comparisons easier and rules easier to apply.

How many times should a product name be repeated in a 30-second spot? Five times. How many exposures to a spot are required to be effective? Three. And so on and so on. As soon as the 30-second spot was treated as an interchangeable unit, it started running out of steam. And into trouble.

In the United States, viewers are subjected to 52 minutes of promotional material during a typical three-hour block of prime time. That's up 8 percent from 2000 and 36 percent from 1991. The average length of commercial breaks has grown as well, jumping 41 percent from 1998 to 2003.

But let's not write more rules. This crazy clutter spells the end of the lazy default to the 30-second spot, but it doesn't mean a fantastic 30-second spot cannot still be created.

In the Attention Age, people value their time. They don't want to hand over 30 seconds of it without getting something back. And what do they want in return? An idea to talk about or open-hearted laughter, to be touched, informed or excited.

The television screen remains a fantastic way to reach the most people fast. Why? sisomo. Thirty seconds has always been too long to watch something boring—but for something fresh and engaging, every second counts.

Television has been an inventive, creative, inspiring medium. For much of the world it still is. But to hold its place today it needs sisomojo—with extra *joie de vivre*. New lengths, new formats, new target possibilities and new interactivity coming at us fast. Surprise and excitement, experimentation and risk.

The Screen Age puts out the welcome mat for every cool idea.

7

"Emerging markets are irrelevant to the future of television."

Emerging markets in China, India, Brazil and Russia are proving faster, more connected and more demanding than anyone dreamed—and they love television. Today households are more likely to possess a television than a telephone.

There are 1.7 billion people in the world belonging to what the Worldwatch Institute calls the consumer class. That means they have a relatively high standard of living. Amazingly, there are more of them than the total number of people alive at the beginning of the twentieth century.

What's interesting about this consumer class is that the biggest number of them, 494 million, live in East Asia and the Pacific, with the next largest share in Europe. The United States comes in third with 271 million people.

The future of television will be played out in emerging countries. China is already the world's fifth-largest advertising market and 75 percent of advertising expenditure goes into television. Every household in urban areas has at least one television set, making China one of the world's most dense media markets.

But television is not only central to economic giants. While an estimated 4 billion people—or two-thirds of the world's population—are numbered amongst the poorest, their access to television keeps growing. In some countries, television viewing rates are just as high in rural as in urban areas because of viewing in groups and communities. The challenge is for television to remain relevant for viewers when so much content is imported. Countries such as Cape Verde and Djibouti import more than 90 percent of their programs, but prosperity tends to come hand-in-hand with more local content.

THE
sisomo
BILLIONS

SOME FACTS AND FIGURES ABOUT SISOMO

Google™

sisomo billions   **Search**   Advanced Search
Preferences

Search: ● the web

Web

1.5 billion mobile phones are in use worldwide
www.**sisomo**.com/sight/sound/motion.htm - 20k - Cached - Similar pages

Consumers worldwide spent **$16.2 billion** on digital television sets and set-top boxes in 2004
www.**sisomo**.com/sight/sound/motion.htm - 20k - Cached - Similar pages

In the US, box office takings are around **$9.5 billion** annually - [Translate this page]
www.**sisomo**.com/sight/sound/motion.htm - 20k - Cached - Similar pages

Sales for video game hardware, software and accessories were **$9.9 billion** in 2004
www.**sisomo**.com/sight/sound/motion.htm - 20k - Cached - Similar pages

The global market for mobile phone games was around **$2.6 billion** in 2005
www.**sisomo**.com/sight/sound/motion.htm - 20k - Cached - Similar pages

It is estimated that by 2008, the global mobile-entertainment market will be worth more than **$27 billion**
www.**sisomo**.com/sight/sound/motion.htm - 20k - Cached - Similar pages
[More results from www.saatchikevin.com]

14.2 billion video streams were served in 2004
www.**sisomo**.com/sight/sound/motion.htm - 20k - Cached - Similar pages

Each month in 2005, **3 billion** text messages were sent
www.**sisomo**.com/sight/sound/motion.htm - 20k - Cached - Similar pages

In 2004, consumers worldwide spent **$51.6 billion** buying and renting home video products (52 percent US, 48 percent rest of the world)
www.**sisomo**.com/sight/sound/motion.htm - 20k - Cached - Similar pages

Television is by far the biggest advertising medium in the US, capturing about **$65 billion** of annual spending
www.**sisomo**.com/sight/sound/motion.htm - 20k - Cached - Similar pages

Kodak estimated that people used their digital cameras to snap about **70 billion** photos in 2005
www.**sisomo**.com/sight/sound/motion.htm - 20k - Cached - Similar pages

Online retail sales in the United States hit **$141.4 billion** in 2004
www.**sisomo**.com/sight/sound/motion.htm - 20k - Cached - Similar pages

Ring tone sales hit **$4 billion** worldwide in 2004 - [Translate this page]
www.**sisomo**.com/sight/sound/motion.htm - 20k - Cached - Similar pages

Google Image Search indexes more than **1 billion** images
www.**sisomo**.com/sight/sound/motion.htm - 20k - Cached - Similar pages

The worldwide Internet population hit more than **1 billion** in 2005
www.**sisomo**.com/sight/sound/motion.htm - 20k - Cached - Similar pages

[PDF] eBay listed **1.8 billion** items for sale in 2005
www.**sisomo**.com/sight/sound/motion.htm - 20k - Cached - Similar pages

The number of web pages exceeds **600 billion**. That's 100 pages for everyone alive
www.**sisomo**.com/sight/sound/motion.htm - 20k - Cached - Similar pages

 ▶

Result Page: 1 2 3 4 5 6 7   **Next**

---

sisomo billions   (Search)

Search within results | Language Tools | Search Tips | Dissatisfied? Help us improve

---

'On television sets, on mobile phone screens and on screens in-store, sisomo is not just a way to deliver great content. It is an attitude, a state of mind, a way of thinking with the heart and feeling with the brain.'

5 Use sisomo to make a music video
of your favorite song using whatever
resources you have.

4 Sign up for the latest, fastest, cheapest
home broadband deal from your telcom.

3 Somewhere in your organization,
there is information just waiting to
be sisomoed. Find it. sisomo it. Fast.

2 Sign up for a multiplayer online game.
Start a second life in a sisomo world.

1 Book a holiday in Akihabara, Tokyo.
Prepare for the sisomotherlode!

CHAPTER 9

Tell me a story...

How sisomo creates compelling stories for Lovemarks

By Kevin Roberts

> "Everything is held together with stories. That is all that is holding us together, stories and compassion."
>
> Barry Holstun Lopez, writer

sisomo tells stories on screen. Human beings have always needed stories as a way to shape their lives and to give them excitement and meaning. sisomo adds the rush of Sight, Sound and Motion. It enhances and enriches the simplest story. It can also clarify and draw us into the most complex one.

Stories are creating new excitement in the market. For much of the last century, stories were relegated to the world of entertainment. Fun and exciting, but of no relevance to business. Business was firmly fixed on the strict logic of management and control. To be avoided at all costs: the "I's" and the "E's." "I" for Ideas, Imagination, Intuition, Insight and Inspiration. "E" for Enchantment, Excitement, Emotion, Empathy and Edge.

In the twenty-first century, the status of stories is being transformed. Their ability to inspire people and to connect with consumers has begun to put them at the heart of business.

And new roles for stories are being invented. Creating preference, communicating new products, defining difference.

Stories have become the constant pulse as companies set out to ignite emotion in business.

At Saatchi & Saatchi, we have always understood the power of storytelling to create deep emotional connections. The best stories evolve and endure with characters we get to know, icons we recognize anywhere and an exciting sense of the future. This is why we have put great stories at the heart of creating Lovemarks.

Lovemarks are the brands, events, experiences and places that people love. Not just like or admire, but love. Passionately. Only Lovemarks explain how to inspire Loyalty Beyond Reason.

Stories, sisomo and Lovemarks are joined at the hip when it comes to long-term emotional connections. Each powerful in its own right, when they go out to play together they become irresistible.

The New Age of Storytelling

Storytelling was always the way societies passed on ideas and information. Stories educated and warned, amazed and entertained. Take the New Zealand Maori. Without writing, the art of oral storytelling kept the society together over centuries.

In the last 100 years, the sheer volume of information to be communicated has overwhelmed traditional modes of storytelling. The role of storyteller lost status and stories were demoted to entertainment.

My belief is that a new, great age of storytelling is at its beginning. Others believe this too.

> "The highest-paid person in the first half of the next century will be the 'storyteller.' The value of products will depend on the story they tell."
>
> Rolf Jensen, "The Dream Society"

I believe that stories are our way through information overload, and that the screen is their natural home. When stories are set against information, the story wins.

The New Storytellers

To tell Lovemarks stories with sisomo on screen demands a new breed of creativity. We used to call it the combination of the left brain and the right brain. Now we simply call it the sisomo brain. sisomo storytellers need:

1. A love of the screen, whether it is on a television set or a mobile phone, in a mediaplex or on a computer.

2. The ability to visualize stories told on screens the size of a matchbox through to screens the size of a house.

3. The skill to combine Sight, Sound and Motion with innovation and imagination as well as accuracy and attention to the last detail.

4. The clarity to navigate through multiple sequences of events and actions so that we can understand where the story has been and where it may take us.

5. A passion for the "what if" questions. The questions that entertain new possibilities and stimulate new ideas.

6. The conviction that the screen offers a relevant and emotional environment for the greatest stories.

7. Access to a rich store of stories. People have been sharing stories for thousands of years. The new sisomo storytellers respect and love this repertoire as well as transform it with relevance and insight.

8. Perspective. It is the golden age of the editor, sifting and filtering and putting together the perfect, relevant ideas and insights in a compelling sequence.

9. An inquiring and curious mind, an appreciation of how the past, present and future can be blended.

10. Judgment. The ability to step up and find out what really happened. And the energy to keep searching to reveal ideas and meanings that might otherwise remain hidden.

11. The new storytellers will need great job titles to reflect what they do: Idea Navigator. Information Designer. Action Architect. Signposter. Fact Finder. Choreographer. Orchestrator. Magician. Guardian of Myths and Legends…

IN THE AGE OF INFORMATION OVERLOAD, WHAT DIFFERENCE CAN A STORY MAKE?

Information	A story
Fills you up	Moves you on
Facts	Acts
Citing	Exciting
Reams	Dreams
Promotional	Emotional
Static	Dramatic
Check lists	Casts of characters
Compiling	Compelling
Annotated	Animated
Feeding the brain	Touching the heart
Tables	Fables
Expires	Inspires

TRUMAN HOUSE

What Makes A Great Story?

- GREAT STORIES TOUCH US. They connect with our own desires and experiences and what we care about.

- GREAT STORIES ARE CONTAGIOUS. The itch to pass on a great story is almost unbearable. Stories have to be shared.

- GREAT STORIES ARE CLOAKED IN CREDIBILITY. They make practical sense, intuitive sense, emotional sense.

- GREAT STORIES CONNECT WITH THE EMOTIONS. Genuine, compelling emotion drives every story.

- GREAT STORIES SURPRISE AND DELIGHT. They are infinitely capable of the unexpected. It's not just about novelty and revelations, but about creativity and emotional truth.

- GREAT STORIES HAVE CONTEXT. Whether it's a fairy tale or a business lesson, stories weave facts and events together so we understand their bigger meaning.

- GREAT STORIES ARE FAST WORKERS. They get in ahead of our rationalizations and logic with their own compelling truth.

- GREAT STORIES ARE CRAFTED. We all like stories to be recounted with skill and effort.

- GREAT STORIES MAKE US LAUGH. Humor disarms us and opens us up to new ideas.

- GREAT STORIES TEACH US TO BE SMART. Through great stories we learn to spot disinformation in an instant. Shoddy stories reinforce prejudice and hide the truth.

- GREAT STORIES INTRODUCE US TO GREAT CHARACTERS. People we want to spend time with.

- GREAT STORIES OPEN US UP TO OTHER WORLDS. Welcome to the world of the imagination, to new geographies, to new realities.

The Craft of Telling Stories

Storytelling skills are essential to creating sisomo on screen and creating Lovemarks.

Most great stories follow a simple idea: what happens next? This is true of stories from Shakespeare to "Batman," from "The Lion King" to "Father & Son," my favorite television commercial of all time, created for our client, Telecom New Zealand.

Are there simple rules for telling compelling stories? I'm with the English writer, W. Somerset Maugham, who said, "There are three rules for writing the novel. Unfortunately, no one knows what they are."

However, I do know there are three essentials for creating Lovemarks. Mystery, Sensuality and Intimacy. And I also know that these same three qualities are crucial to sisomo and exactly what you look for in a fantastic, engaging story.

Start with Mystery. In developing Lovemarks, we discovered that Mystery taps into dreams, it draws on great myths and icons, puts the past, present and future together and (no surprise here) Mystery tells great stories. Mystery is what engages us, feeds our curiosity and makes us want more.

Mystery's questions are: who is going to do what, how, and when?

Sensuality draws on the five senses of sight, hearing, smell, taste and touch. This is how we experience the world. sisomo engages directly with Sight and Sound, but the power of sisomo can make us believe we are experiencing the other three as well. Looking forward, our imaginations are being stimulated by touch screens already, so the idea of taste and smell via screens now feels like an exciting prospect for new storytelling rather than an idle dream.

Sensuality's questions are: how does the world of the story touch each of the senses?

Intimacy is shaped by the deeply emotional qualities of passion, empathy and commitment. These three are all aroused by stories, but empathy is the most powerful. Who hasn't been touched personally by a story? Who hasn't wondered how it was possible for a line of dialogue or a gesture to feel so familiar? sisomo brings intimacy even closer so we see ourselves face to face.

Intimacy's questions are: what will make this audience feel as though this is their story?

How to sisomo Great Stories

The explosion of sisomo on the screen is transforming the possibilities for storytelling. Where once television and the movies had the field to themselves, the allure of screens everywhere is demanding new story skills.

As television becomes more game-like, as mobile phones become more television-like, and as store screens become more movie-like, storytelling is evolving as well.

The march of on-demand television is an opportunity, not a threat. As consumers have more choice, the stories have to be better. The development of sisomo content will become the obsession of creative communicators everywhere.

Some ideas to get you started.

GET EMOTIONAL

Whether you are telling your story on a phone or a mega-screen in Times Square, emotion is what will make it memorable and inspiring.

GET PERSONAL

The world being created by sisomo can be a wild and crazy one. "The Economist" asked, "Are games evil?" on its cover. sisomo storytellers are on the front line of a society-wide debate. When is violence too violent? How much sex is OK? Who should play and who should not? Issues all under pressure from different moral standards and different expectations. The way through? A strong sense of personal purpose. Does it make the world a better place? Do what's right.

GET ANIMATED

Sight and Sound are everywhere. Motion sometimes lags behind. The catch-up rule is simple: whatever is static will become animated.

BELIEVE IN THE MAGIC

The screen is a magic medium. It has such power that it can retain interest as it conveys emotions and moods that no other art form can hope to tackle, says Stanley Kubrick.

PLAY WITH MUSIC

Music is a sisomo heavy-lifter. Voices or songs or stunning sound effects make every story come alive. Music creates mood. As Hank Williams Snr. once said, "A song ain't nothin' in the world but a story just wrote with music to it."

GO FOR THE LONG TERM

In advertising it used to be called campaignability. Take it out of ad language and you get to the core of stories: the ability to enthrall an audience not just once, but over and over again. The only test for a television commercial in the sisomo world is: do I want to see it again?

LOVE HUMOR

Humor is an attitude and tone. It's certainly not a one-liner to be used once and thrown away.

CROSS MEDIA

Telling a story in a video game is different than telling a story (even with the same characters and title) as a feature film or 30-second television commercial. If the experiences of the past five years or so tell us anything, it's that the differences don't compete with each other, they inspire each other.

EMBRACE INTERACTIVITY

As television remote controls become more mouse-like, interactivity ramps up. The potential for multi-layered, multi-ending and multi-purpose stories is fantastic. Remember the pick-a-path stories at the beginning of the video game revolution? Events have overtaken this clumsy idea, but the desire for stories that can travel in a multitude of different directions is central to modern storytelling.

SHARE CONTROL, AND LEARN TO LOVE IT

Storytellers will increasingly share control with their listeners, watchers, players.

No two players of a game like "EverQuest," for example, will play the same game or play the same game twice. Why? Because the stories fork and branch with such complexity. The same is true on the web, where traditional narrative often gives way to collage and commentary with a growing emphasis on moving the story along with sisomo.

PUSH YOUR CRAFT

Continuously challenge yourself to exceed your personal best. As software and hardware evolve and the ways to connect them get more enmeshed, as technology gets easier and ordinary people can do more, demands on professional-level skills can only get higher.

COUNT EVERY SECOND

There is increasing pressure on storytellers to keep it short, to chunk it and to be responsive to their audience. How to tell a story in five seconds? To get beyond the transfer of information, the full sisomo repertoire will be demanded. This skill is second nature in advertising, where short films lasting 30 seconds (otherwise known as commercials) have become a staple of television. It was natural that the people with these extreme story skills helped invent the music video. I believe they will also lead the way into our sisomo future.

There is one certainty we can depend on in the decades ahead. People will always relish great stories. The challenge will be in spreading sisomo experiences across all screens to tell those stories with emotion, authenticity, passion and commitment. This is the only way to deserve the ancient and inspirational name of Storyteller.

sisomo brings the global to your local and takes the local to the screens of the world

making the world a better place with sisomo

Our millennium report card
would have to read:

"must do much better."

The list is in plain view:
environmental degradation;
chronic imbalances between
over-consuming rich countries and
depleted, impoverished ones; over
8 million deaths a year from extreme
poverty and disease; suppression
of democracy and basic freedoms;
subjugation of women and children;
human rights abuses; failed states;
underfunding, backtracking and
theft of development aid; weapons
trade; corruption; nepotism;
cronyism; jingoism and the rest.
If countries were people, half of
them would be committed.

The way to change the
world is one person at a
time. The power of one is
unstoppable. There are
few problems we can't
solve if enough people
apply themselves. As
individuals, working together.

So where does sisomo fit?
How can the latest cool gadgets and
amazing screens, entertainment, phones
and games make a real difference? Are they
making the gap between rich and poor
people even more extreme? Or can they
help enable a better world for everyone?

The basic needs in the 50 least-developed
countries of the world are nutrition, health,
education, productivity of agriculture and
investment in infrastructure. Relatively small
investments can deliver massive benefits.
Three million people—mostly children—die
each year from malaria. A $7 anti-malaria
bed net will save a child for five years.

Part of the solution lies in presidents and
prime ministers acting heroically to spread
democratic freedoms and a capitalism of
inclusion. Asia and Africa were in a similar
situation 50 years ago, but Asia escaped from
the vicious cycles thanks to inspired actions
by individuals operating in the political
process. Today Asians are the most intense
consumers and users of sisomo in the world.

The market has a
key role—seeing
possibility where
others see calamity
or exploitation.
Entrepreneurs are
responsible for
the fact that Africa
today has 82 million
mobile phone users.

And technologists
are central. Brilliant
minds have invented
the infrastructure and
sophisticated technologies that have made
sisomo. Television, broadband, mobile
devices of all kinds, the list just keeps getting
longer. You can guarantee that right now,
innovators are working on new, clever and
cheap ways to bring low-cost connectivity
and electricity to the parts of the world that
have none. The bi-annual Saatchi & Saatchi
Award for World Changing Ideas has featured
several innovations designed to improve the
lives of people living entirely without sisomo:

Inspiring examples are the Light Up The World Foundation's ultra-efficient, durable and near-permanent lighting solutions powered by renewable energy for the millions of people in the world without access to electricity; and the low-cost, self-adjusting spectacles invented by Oxford physicist Joshua Silver for the tens of millions of people who need glasses but do not have access to health services. For many people in the world, the prerequisites of sisomo—electricity, vision and so on, are still a dream.

The value of sisomo, as language and as technology, is that it takes the paradigm into human terms. With sisomo we can put emotional engagement at the center, inspiring us to do what's right according to where we live, what our resources are and what opportunities we have available to us.

For those of us in developed nations, sisomo can help bring understanding and urgency to the challenges the planet faces, followed by the determination to take sustained and focused action. For the 2 billion people in emerging nations, sisomo can enable business and education opportunities, build self-esteem and confidence as well as inspire aspirations for a better life.

Take a wise saying we are all familiar with. **"Give a man a fish and you feed him for a day. Teach a man to fish and you feed his family for a lifetime."**

This makes perfect sense, but the question is, **"What action is needed to make this shift?"**

SISOMO AND TRANSFORMATION

The role of business is to make the world a better place for everyone. For 6.4 billion people. Not one less. It is business that plans and connects the global flow of goods, ideas and experiences. It is business that leads innovation and creates jobs, choices and opportunities.

In a changing world, we need ideas that can maneuver, shape-shift, transform. To face change as a challenge rather than a threat. That's why we need sisomo. sisomo is driving the transformation of communication and media that is central to the transformation of our world.

MEDIA IS (MOSTLY) EVERYWHERE

A television set or a telephone is never far away from most of the world's citizens. It might simply be a single television set in the middle of a village square, but access is access. Ideas can live and do their work anywhere. With sisomo, the barriers of isolation and exclusion can be overcome as the globe shrinks.

MEDIA IS FASTER, CHEAPER

Scale makes the difference. Moore's Law—that computing power and speed doubles every 18 months—has ensured that the technological infrastructure gets faster and cheaper by the day. Metcalfe's Law—that the value of a network rises exponentially every time someone joins—has ensured that sisomo connections are multiplying rapidly.

MEDIA IS GOING LOCAL

The fear that two or three mega-media companies would dominate the world has proved misplaced. The vitality of media at a granular level is irresistible. People want to see themselves and their stories on screen. As television establishes itself in new markets, it is usually followed quickly by a boom in local programming. The Internet is experiencing the same trajectory—as people communicate, transact and relate in their own language and often in their own media space.

The more the technology advances, the more control it offers to consumers. The creation of sisomo content with and by consumers, not just for them, is becoming a reality. The level of sisomo quality a teacher can produce in an average school somewhere in South America would have wowed the professionals ten years ago.

sisomo is following the path of many other technologies, from new seed strains to wind power, and heading out into the world. Can sisomo help make the world a better place? I believe the answer is yes. With inspired consumers and producers, it can.

SISOMO CONNECTS

sisomo brings vibrant images, sounds and actions to isolated communities. The story of the ceramic artists in a Mexican village transforming their roadside stall into a global market via eBay is inspirational. The positive effect of feeling part of local, regional and global communities cannot be overestimated. sisomo is inclusive.

SISOMO EDUCATES

The bar has been raised. We know that education is one of the most powerful forces of change. Now sisomo offers amazing new opportunities for teaching and learning in emerging countries where literacy is a major issue. Take the power of gaming. Still in its infancy, the possibilities it offers for relevant and engaging learning experiences are truly life-changing. Knowledge is power, and sisomo is knowledge in its most compelling form.

SISOMO ENCOURAGES PROSPERITY

There is no question that communications and computing devices enable commerce and access to information and add speed to transactions. Mobile phones play a significant part in promoting bottom-up socioeconomic development, even in the poorest countries. The number of mobile users is growing twice as fast in developing countries as in developed markets. Africa is the fastest growing mobile market in the world.

SISOMO ARTICULATES THE LOCAL

The shared language of sisomo gives access to the richness of cultures we are unlikely to encounter in person. At the same time, it shows the potential of local identities to be extraordinary and compelling.

SISOMO EXPOSES THE GLOBAL

Or it should. According to *The New York Times*, in June, 2005, CNN, Fox News, NBC, MSNBC, ABC and CBS collectively ran 55 times as many stories about the Michael Jackson trial as they ran about genocide in Darfur, Sudan. An estimated 400,000 Sudanese people died as a result of war, disease and starvation. I admire Bono and Bob Geldof for bringing their distinctive form of Irish sisomojo to the television screens to pressure for solutions to poverty.

SISOMO AND THE FUTURE

Young people will create the future of sisomo. They are the most alert to its potential and most responsive to its transforming power.

Look at the numbers. Two billion young people–that's people under 18 years of age–make up about one-third of the world's population. In the least developed nations, these young people can comprise up to half the population.

These 2 billion young people have huge challenges ahead of them. But it has been my experience that the young are more optimistic, more open to the world and more curious than older people.

Wherever they live, young people are shaped more by the media than any generation before them. This has been the case since the 1950s, and the pervasiveness of the media has only become more intense over the decades.

Today there is no doubt. The young are not just the children of the media, they are the children of sisomo.

For where there is sisomo, there is communication and hope, and there are dreams and a possibility for a better world.

ONE—A STAND FOR HUMAN RIGHTS

"ONE is something that people from all backgrounds and political leanings can agree on. There are no sides to take; there's no argument here. There's a wildfire out there and we have the ability to put it out. What are we going to do?" Brad Pitt

In 2005, the ONE Campaign united a million Americans, from heartland to Hollywood. Together they made a stand against extreme poverty and AIDS.

Part of the international Make Poverty History movement, ONE reached out to Americans—not for their money, but their voices—by asking them to sign a declaration on www.one.org.

ONE advocates an increase in humanitarian aid to 1 percent of the US federal budget. This could help:

- Prevent 10 million children from becoming AIDS orphans.

- Provide water to almost 900 million children around the globe.

- Save almost 6.5 million children under five from dying of preventable diseases.

The ONE Campaign was founded by 11 of the nation's leading relief and anti-poverty organizations: Bread for the World, CARE, DATA, International Medical Corps, International Rescue Committee, Mercy Corps, Oxfam America, Plan USA, Save the Children US, World Concern, and World Vision. ONE is supported by the Bill & Melinda Gates Foundation and Sun Microsystems.

The ONE television campaign was created and produced by @radical.media with producers Jon Kamen and Greg Schultz, director Marcus Tomlinson and writer Joe O'Neill. @radical.media is a global media and entertainment company that works alongside most of the world's advertising agencies on commercial production, as well as on the development and production of entertainment projects for network and cable TV, feature films and live theater.

Bono of U2 launched the campaign at the 2005 Technology, Entertainment and Design (TED) conference in Monterey, California. He called on the 800 thought-leaders at TED to deliver 1 billion media impressions of the campaign prior to the G8 conference.

The ONE spot had its global premiere on April 10, 2005, across ABC and global MTV Networks, with MTV USA alone screening the spot 700 times.

Inspired by the TED challenge, Jay Amato, CEO of Viewpoint—a technology company behind some of the most innovative visual experiences on the web and desktops—undertook an unprecedented online public awareness campaign. He coordinated the donation and placement of $5 million of online advertising on behalf of ONE in the lead-up to the 2005 G8.

At peak, Viewpoint delivered 30 million online ads per day for ONE, in 25 different formats consisting of standard, rich media and video advertisements. Viewpoint secured 1.5 billion impressions from 23 donating publishers including AOL, 24/7 Real Media, MSN, Google, MSNBC, *The New York Times*, About.com, Burst! Media, Gamespot, Accuweather.com, Right Media, ValueClick, CBS.com, CBS News and UPN.

ONE continues at www.one.org, where you can sign the ONE Declaration to make poverty history.

"One by one they step forward. A nurse. A teacher. A homemaker. And lives are saved. But the problem is enormous. Every three seconds one person dies. Another three seconds, one more. The situation is so desperate in parts of Africa, Asia, even America, that aid groups, like they did for the tsunami, are uniting as one, acting as one. We can beat extreme poverty, starvation, AIDS. But we need your help. One more person, letter, voice, will mean the difference between life or death for millions of people. So please join together. By working together, Americans have an unprecedented opportunity. We can make history. We can start to make poverty history. One, by one, by one. Please visit us at www.one.org. We're not asking for your money, we're asking for your voice."

ONE THE CAMPAIGN TO MAKE POVERTY HISTORY

WWW.SISOMO.COM

Learn about Sight, Sound and Motion in the real
world. Start with sporting events and stage shows.
Take your insights to the world of the screen.

Attend to the last detail. sisomo demands precision
whether you're creating images or soundscapes,
animating or programming, structuring content
or writing with perfect punctuation.

Tap the wisdom of the young. They live
and breathe sisomo. They love to share
their knowledge and their delight.

Get involved with spreading sisomo in schools
and communities. They need action and energy.
Turn digital divides into digital dividends.

Know when to switch off. Go to a park, breathe
fresh air, read a novel, make love, enjoy the
real world...never be a sisomo bore!

sisomo backstage

A new word for a new world

Sight, Sound and Motion have been a powerful combination since humans first banged on a drum and got up to dance. The television screen took sisomo to new heights, but now screens everywhere are talking a new sisomo language.

"Great program, great sisomo."

"Loved the way she sisomoed the introduction."

"Where's the sisomo edge to that idea?"

"The whole show was incredibly sisomoed. What a rollercoaster ride."

"That story sisomoed up really well."

"We're sisomo-capable."

"We're sisomoing all our ideas."

"Anything you can see is sisomoable with music and some action."

"He can make the ordinary, extraordinary—a real sisomover."

A sisomo reading list

Christopher Booker, *The Seven Basic Plots: Why We Tell Stories*, Continuum, 2004.

John Seely Brown and Paul Duguid, *The Social Life of Information*, Harvard Business School Press, 2000.

Stephen Denning, *The Leader's Guide to Storytelling: Mastering the Art and Discipline of Business Narrative*, Jossey-Bass, 2005.

Joel Garreau, *Radical Evolution: The Promise and Peril of Enhancing Our Minds, Our Bodies—and What It Means to Be Human*, Doubleday, 2004.

Kenneth J. Gergen, *The Saturated Self: Dilemmas of Identity in Contemporary Life*, Basic Books, 1991.

Todd Gitlin, *Media Unlimited: How the Torrent of Images and Sounds Overwhelms Our Lives*, Henry Holt and Company, 2001.

Joseph Jaffe, *Life After the 30-Second Spot: Energize Your Brand with a Bold Mix of Alternatives to Traditional Advertising*, Wiley, 2005.

Rolf Jensen, *The Dream Society: How the Coming Shift from Information to Imagination Will Transform Your Business*, McGraw-Hill, 1999.

Steven Johnson, *Mind Wide Open: Your Brain and the Neuroscience of Everyday Life*, Scribner, 2004.

Steven Johnson, *Everything Bad Is Good for You: How Today's Popular Culture Is Actually Making Us Smarter*, Riverhead Books, 2005.

Pat Kane, *The Play Ethic: A Manifesto for a Different Way of Living*, McMillan, 2004.

Lawrence Lessig, *Free Culture: How Big Media Uses Technology and the Law to Lock Down Culture and Control Creativity*, The Penguin Press, 2004.

Martin Lindstrom, *Brand Sense: Build Powerful Brands Through Touch, Taste, Smell, Sight, and Sound*, Free Press, 2005.

Jerry Mander, *Four Arguments for the Elimination of Television*, Perennial, 1978.

Marshall McLuhan, *Understanding Media*, Routledge & Kegan Paul Ltd., 1964.

Nicholas Negroponte, *Being Digital*, Vintage Books, 1996.

Donald Norman, *Emotional Design: Why We Love (Or Hate) Everyday Things*, Basic Books, 2004.

Mark Pesce, *The Playful World: How Technology Is Transforming Our Imagination*, Ballantine Books, 2000.

Daniel H. Pink, *A Whole New Mind: Moving from the Information Age to the Conceptual Age*, Riverhead Books, 2005.

Virginia Postrel, *The Substance of Style: How the Rise of Aesthetic Value Is Remaking Commerce, Culture and Consciousness*, HarperCollins, 2003.

Byron Reeves and Clifford Nass, *The Media Equation: How People Treat Computers, Television, and New Media Like Real People and Places*, Cambridge University Press, 1996.

Roger C. Schank, *Tell Me a Story: Narrative and Intelligence*, Northwestern University Press, 1995.

Michael Schrage, *Serious Play: How the World's Best Companies Simulate to Innovate*, Harvard Business School Press, 2000.

Tom Shone, *Blockbuster: How Hollywood Learned to Stop Worrying and Love the Summer*, Simon & Schuster, 2004.

James Surowiecki, *The Wisdom of Crowds: Why Many are Smarter than the Few and How Collective Wisdom Shapes Business, Economics, Societies and Nations*, Doubleday, 2004.

John Thackara, *In the Bubble: Designing in a Complex World*, The MIT Press, 2005.

David Thomson, *The Whole Equation: A History of Hollywood*, Knopf, 2004.

Visionaire, in particular *No. 24: Light, No. 27: Movement* and *No. 38: Love*, Visionaire Publishing.

David L. Weiner, *What Your Mind Knows, But Isn't Telling You*, Prometheus Books, 2005.

Thomas de Zengotita, *Mediated: How the Media Shapes Your World and the Way You Live In It*, Bloomsbury, 2005.

Photo credits

Page 2-3: Star trails over Eiger, Mönch and Jungfrau mountains in Switzerland.
Photographer: Frank Lukasseck/iStockPhotos

Page 8-9: An audience watches a 3-D movie at a theater in Jacksonville, Florida.
Image: SuperStocks Studio

Page 10-11: A Buddhist monk at the Myoren-ji Temple in Kyoto, Japan.
Photographer: Michael S. Yamashita/CORBIS

Page 12-13: Asian ribbon dancers.
Copyright: Jocelyn Lin

Page 18: While waiting for his flight, a passenger watches a DVD on a portable player at LAX.
Photographer: J. Romanov

Page 20-21: A New York crowd watches the coronation of Queen Elizabeth II on June 2, 1953.
Image: Bettmann/CORBIS

Page 25: Ginger Rogers and Fred Astaire in a dance scene from the 1938 Irving Berlin musical *Carefree*, an RKO Radio Picture.
Image: Bettmann/CORBIS

Page 27: Seven sheriffs who toted guns in Warner Bros.-produced Westerns for ABC TV. The most well-known are: Will Hutchins, Sugarfoot; Peter Brown, Lawman; Jack Kelly, Maverick; Wayne Preston, Colt 45; and John Russell, Lawman.
Image: Bettmann/CORBIS

Page 30-31: A Western being filmed on a movie set.
Photographer: Adam Woolfitt/CORBIS

Page 32-33: A scene being filmed in Mexico City for one of the daily episodes of the *televisa novel* (television soap opera) *Infierno en el Paraíso*.
Photographer: Keith Dannemiller/CORBIS

Page 34-35: A crowd watches Pope John Paul II reciting the rosary from inside St. Patrick's Cathedral in Manhattan during his 1995 visit to the United States.
Photographer: Mark Peterson/CORBIS

Page 36-37: Two children watch television in Singapore.
Photographer: Jack Hollingsworth/CORBIS

Page 38-39: Scene from PlayStation's *Gran Turismo 4*. All manufacturers, cars, names, brands and associated imagery featured in this game are trademarks and/or copyrighted materials of their respective owners.

Page 40: Lightbulb and moth.
Image: Blink Creative/iStockPhotos

Page 42: At Tranquility Base, Apollo 11 commander Neil Armstrong's first footstep leaves its mark on the moon's surface, July 20, 1969.
Image: Bettmann/CORBIS

Page 43: A young woman uses a touch screen pay phone in Dublin.
Image: CORBIS

Page 43: In 1994, ABC News films O.J. Simpson in his Ford Bronco as he is chased by police along Interstate 405 in Los Angeles.
Photographer: Rick Maiman/CORBIS

Page 44: An Internet connection allows a Los Angeles exerciser to use the screen while working out at the gym.
Photographer: Frederic Neema/CORBIS

Page 45: A break dancer holds tight to his mobile phone.
Photographer: Edward Bock/CORBIS

Page 46: Playing games in a video arcade.
Photographer: DiMaggio/Kalish/CORBIS

Page 47: A Japanese woman is filmed emailing a photograph on her mobile phone to a friend standing next to her.
Photographer: J. Romanov

Page 48: Actors on the set of *Café Chill*, a Pakistani TV comedy series.
Photographer: Ed Kashi/CORBIS

Page 48: People concentrate on computer screens at the Bibliotheca Alexandrina in Egypt.
Photographer: Sandro Vannini/CORBIS

Page 49: A fan at a Minnesota Vikings game watches TV to get a better look at the action on the field.
Photographer: Annie Griffiths Belt/CORBIS

Page 70-71: Times Square, New York City.
Photographer: Ruby Sulgan/iStockPhotos

Page 74: The Red Bull Air Race website.
Source: www.redbullairrace.com

Page 74: Peter Jackson on the cover of *The Hollywood Reporter.*

Page 74: Visitors to the Frank Gehry–designed Sky Church view images and listen to sounds.
Image: Sorbo Robert/CORBIS

Page 75: Promotional graphic for the television series, 24.
Source: http://tvspielfilm.msn.de

Page 75: Poster for the television series, *The Sopranos.*
Source: ilya.blackbox.ru/

Page 75: Marc Newson phone for Talby Mobile.
Source: www.marc-newson.com

Page 76: Times Square, New York.
Photographer: Brian Joseph

Page 76: New Zealand All Blacks on a stadium screen.
Images: Brian Joseph and Ross Land/Fotopress Ltd., with permission of the New Zealand Rugby Union.

Page 77: Characters from the video game *Fable.*
Source: www.xbox.com

Page 77: Bono sings at the Zoo TV concert in 1992.
Source: www.u2.to.pl

Page 78: Homepage of the New Zealand Edge website.
Source: www.nzedge.com

Page 78: *The Hire*, a BMW short film.
Source: www.bmwfilms.com

Page 78: Amanda Congdon, presenter of the vlog *Rocketboom.*
Source: rocketboom.com/vlog

Page 79: *All is Full of Love*, Björk's music video created by Chris Cunningham.
Source: blog.livedoor.jp/

Page 79: Selection of Hannspree screens.
Source: www.hannspree.com

Page 80-81: Person holding a gaming device.
Photographer: blende64/iStockPhotos

Page 82-83: A fan takes a picture of the big screen showing a rugby match between the New Zealand All Blacks and the British and Irish Lions.
Photographer: Kane McPherson

Page 84-85: A couple watch their portable television set outdoors.
Photographer: Pete Seaward/CORBIS

Page 86-87: Horses at a Hong Kong track speed past a giant screen presenting their race.
Photographer: Massimo Mastrorillo/CORBIS

Page 88-89: In Louis, Missouri, a man relaxes watching television.
Image: FK PHOTO/CORBIS

Page 90-91: Using a battery-powered set, two men in Cambodia take time off for karaoke.
Photographer: Reza; Webistan/CORBIS

Page 92-93: Doctors reviewing non-invasive surgery techniques in Silver Spring, Maryland.
Photographer: Richard T. Nowitz/CORBIS

Page 97: Abandoned television.
Photographer: Leon Rose/Plump Studio

Page 100-101: A Tibetan woman in a photography studio in Lhasa.
Photographer: Owen Franken/CORBIS

Page 102-103: A couple living near Xian in the Shaanxi Province of China watch television in their living room.
Photographer: Carl & Ann Purcell/CORBIS

Page 104-105: A Peruvian woman carrying a child on her back watches television through a window.
Image: Gustavo Gilabert/CORBIS

Page 106-107: The community television set in the small village of La Victoire, Ivory Coast.
Photographer: James P. Blair/National Geographic

Page 108-109: Campers in the desert in Kuwait with their television.
Photographer: Joe Raedle/Reportage Getty Images

Page 110-111: TV antennas and roofs in Bairro Alto, Lisbon, Portugal.
Photographer: Doug Scott/iStockPhotos

Page 122-123: A theater audience settles down for the main show.
Image: Getty Images

Page 128: The video crew watches insurance salesman Truman Burbank (Jim Carrey) who is unaware his life is being recorded as a television show, in the 1998 movie *The Truman Show*.
Image: CORBIS SYGMA

Page 130: A man holds tight to his chair as he is filmed for a television advertisement.
Photographer: Layne Kennedy/CORBIS

Page 132: Albanians in Kosovo use parabolic dishes to receive Albanian television.
Photographer: G. Mastrullo/Grazia Neri/CORBIS Sygma

Page 133-137: Aerial view of Great Barrier Reef, Australia.
Image: Grant Faint/The Image Bank

Page 138-139: Actors and musicians give a face and voice to making poverty history in the ONE Campaign—www.one.org.
Photography: Marcus Tomlinson, @radical.media

Page 140-141: Nancy Reagan waves to her husband, President Ronald Reagan, in a video conference.
Photographer: Wally McNamee/CORBIS

Page 142-143: Watching the sun rise.
Photographer: John Brown/STONE Getty Images

Page 144-145: A camel caravan crosses the desert.
Image: Firefly Productions/CORBIS

Page 146-147: Children splashing in water.
Photographer: Roger De La Harpe; Gallo Images/ CORBIS

Page 148-149: An extreme skier performs a backflip.
Image: CORBIS

Page 150-151: Olodum, the most popular carnival band in Salvador, gives one of their weekly performances.
Photographer: Floris Leeuwenberg/CORBIS

Page 152-153: Stuntman Greg Brazzell drives a car into a delivery truck loaded with bottled water, during a stunt for the motion picture *Ripperman*.
Photographer: Rick Doyle/CORBIS

Page 156-157: A giant screen picks up the action in the World Cup of soccer.
Photographer: Wally McNamee/CORBIS

Page 159: Visitors walk under the dramatic image of a music video being played on an outdoor screen at the Mori Center in Tokyo.
Photographer: J. Romanov

Inside back cover: Screen lights.
Photographer: Kane McPherson

Inside back cover: Kevin Roberts.
Photographer: M. Stockill

Illustration credits

Page 36-37: Kids watching TV with cartoons.
Illustrator: Scott Wilson, mobile: +64 24 876 013

Page 50-51: The Family of Screens title page.
Illustrator: Kane McPherson, email: kanemc@mac.com

Page 52-69: The Family of Screens characters.
Illustrator: Jon Chapman-Smith, Fuman Creative.

sisomo sources

SISOMO: THE FUTURE ON SCREEN

Page 16: Books like Robert Ornstein, *The Right Mind: Making Sense of the Hemispheres*, Harvest Books, 1997, and Daniel H. Pink, *A Whole New Mind: Moving from the Information Age to the Conceptual Age*, Riverhead Books, 2005, are two of many that track the rise of the right brain.

GREAT SISOMOMENTS

This highly selective sisomo timeline is sourced from The Media History Project (School of Journalism and Mass Communication, College of Liberal Arts, University of Minnesota), The American Film Institute, Internet Movie Database, and, always, Wikipedia.

Page 26: The Gartner Group made the projection of 3 billion mobile users by 2010; Xi Guohua, Chinese vice minister of information industry, was quoted on the number of users in China, Yahoo! News, June 28, 2005; the Wireless World Forum calculates the statistics for Africa.

Page 28: David Farber's Interesting-People list recorded the launch of Pizza Hut online ordering on August 22, 1994; and Shop.org and Forrester Research track progress in *The State of Retailing Online 8.0.*

Page 28: Wikipedia tells the story of the weblog; and the Pew Internet and American Life Project, *The State of Blogging*, May 2005, nails the numbers.

Page 29: Digital Entertainment Group, January 2005 and *CE Ownership and Market Potential*, Consumer Electronics Association, 2005.

Page 29: Frances Gleeson, "Camera Phones Outsell Digital Cameras," Environmental News Network, September 22, 2003.

Page 29: National Bureau of Statistics of China calculates the number of television viewers based on 2002 data.

Page 29: Video Software Dealers Association reported that 28.2 million DVDs were rented during the week ending June 15, 2003, while 27.3 million VHS cassettes were rented.

SISOMO ON SCREEN: THE BIG ATTRACTION
Page 41: Stephen Bottomore, "The Panicking Audience? Early Cinema and the 'Train Effect,'" *Historical Journal of Film, Radio and Television*, Vol. 19, No. 2, 1999.

Page 41: Donald Calne, *Within Reason: Rationality and Human Behavior*, Vintage Books, 2000.

Page 42: David Thomson explores the paradox of intimacy in *The Whole Equation: A History of Hollywood*, Knopf, 2004.

Page 42: Thirty-three percent of households in the United States owned a home theater system in January, 2005, up from 21 percent in January, 2000, according to a Consumer Electronics Association survey.

Page 43: Consumer Electronics Association draws on the National Kitchen & Bath Association Survey in *Five Technologies to Watch*, November, 2005.

Page 43: The number of sleepers with phones turned on was revealed by Gary Silverman in "Cell Phones to Replace TV as Prime Advertising Medium," *Financial Times*, July 4, 2005.

Page 44: Consumer Electronics Association lists the most desired electronic gifts.

Page 45: National Institute of Media and the Family counts the number of Americans watching television with dinner.

Page 45: Peter Francese, "Well Enough Alone," *American Demographics*, November 1, 2003, scopes the solo life.

Page 45: Wataru Maruyama looks at the potential of the next generation of games in "Get Your Game On," *Digital World Magazine*, April, 2005.

Page 45: The size of the global games industry is added up by Robert MacMillan, "The Video Game Industry's Strategy Guide," *Washington Post*, May 20, 2005; the number of people playing multiplayer online games is noted by Mark Wallace, "The Game is Virtual. The Profit is Real," *The New York Times*, May 29, 2005; Olga Kharif investigates mobile phone games in "Taking Video Games to the Next Level," *Business Week*, May 9, 2005; David Becker, "*Halo 2* Clears Record $125 Million in First Day," C/Net, November 10, 2004.

Page 45: Gerhard Florin on queuing as a sign of passion in "EA to Take on Film and TV Giants," BBC News, January 17, 2005.

Page 46: Anthony Breznican, "Spielberg, Zemeckis Say Video Games, Films Could Merge," *USA Today*, September 16, 2005.

Page 46: Steven Johnson, *Everything Bad Is Good for You: How Today's Popular Culture Is Actually Making Us Smarter*, Riverhead Books, 2005, makes the connection between games and reading.

Page 46: www.americasarmy.com has the army's online recruitment game and its background.

Page 46: The amount of time spent watching television is recorded in "Study Finds Japanese Watch Most TV," Reuters, April 12, 2005.

Page 47: The new interest of economists in happiness is discussed in Claudia Wallis, "The New Science of Happiness: What Makes the Human Heart Sing?" *Time*, January 17, 2005; and Benedict Carey, "What Makes People Happy? TV, Study Says," *The New York Times*, December 2, 2004.

Page 47: Mark Caro discusses the links between entertainment and sport in "Which is More Thrilling: Drama in Sports or Arts?" *Chicago Tribune*, April 1, 2005.

Page 48: The story of remote controls is told by Christine Rosen in "The Age of Egocasting," *The New Atlantis*, Fall 2004/Winter 2005.

Page 48: The interaction of different media is discussed in "Internet Feeding, not Beating, Other Media," *Variety*, April 18, 2005.

THE FAMILY OF SCREENS
Page 61: The number of consumers with DVD players in their cars is noted in "Movie Downloading Awareness Grows; While Many Watch On the Go," *Ipsos-Insight*, June 15, 2005.

SISOMO IN ACTION
Page 76: Marc Newson was quoted in "The Shape of Things to Come," CNN, July 5, 2005.

Page 77: Jon Pardes captures U2's great television concert in "High-Tech and Nostalgia in U2 Show," *The New York Times*, August 15, 1992.

Page 77: Wikipedia tracks the evolution of Animutation using Flash.

Page 79: Jon Caramanica looks at the development of music videos in "I Screen, You Screen: the New Age of the Music Video," *The New York Times*, July 31, 2005.

WHERE DOES THIS LEAVE TELEVISION?
Page 109: Daya Kishan Thussu, *Electronic Empires: Global Media and Local Resistance*, Arnold Publishers, 1998; and Bella Thomas, "What the World's Poor Watch on TV," *World Press Review*, March 2003.

SEVEN URBAN MYTHS ABOUT TELEVISION
Page 112: "PricewaterhouseCoopers Says Entertainment and Media Industry in Strongest Position Since 2000," media release, June 22, 2005, projects that television's value as an advertising medium will rise to $186 billion in 2009.

Page 112: In *Digital Media 2005*, the Consumer Electronics Association tracks the growth of the home theater; and Michael Krantz, "Television That Leaps off the Screen," *The New York Times*, July 3, 2005, counts the number of lines in 3-D television.

Page 113: The amount of time spent away from home is calculated by Simmons Market Research Bureau and Mark Mays, Clear Channel Communications, and quoted in Tom Lowry, "On-the-Go Consumers," *Business Week Online*, July 12, 2004.

Page 113: Bradley Johnson, "How US Consumers Spend Their Time," *Ad Age*, May 2, 2005, sums up the television viewing statistics from the American Time Use Survey; and Victoria Rideout, Donald F. Roberts and Ulla G. Fochr focus on the media use of young people in *Generation M: Media in the Lives of 8-18-Year-Olds*, Kaiser Family Foundation, 2005.

Page 113: www.fifa.com records World Cup Final audiences; but note the caution of numbers guy Carl Bialik, "When it Comes to TV Stats, Viewer Discretion is Advised," *Wall Street Journal*, July 21, 2005.

Page 114: David C. Tice, *The Digital Dilemma*, Knowledgenetworks, Spring/Summer 2005, digs beneath the surface of consumers' digital media attitudes and buying choices.

Page 115: Constance L. Hays, "Wal-Mart is Upgrading its Vast In-Store Television Network," *The New York Times*, February 21, 2005.

Page 115: The possibilities of in-store screens are imagined by *Captive Audience Networks: Enhancing the Retail Experience*, How and Why Group, May 2004.

Page 117: The volume of promotional material on television is added up in *Advertising Environment Study*, PhaseOne Communications, 2003.

Page 118: "State of the World 2004," World Watch Institute defines the consumer class and Nielsen Media Research adds up China. Levels of imported content are noted by Bella Thomas, "What the World's Poor Watch on TV," *World Press Review*, March 2003.

THE SISOMO BILLIONS: SOME FACTS AND FIGURES ABOUT SISOMO
Mobile phones: International Telecommunication Union.

Digital TV sets: Katherine Meyer, "Gadgets," *The Wall Street Journal*, May 6, 2005.

Box office: NATO (National Association of Theater Owners).

Video game sales: NPD Funworld 2005.

Olga Kharif, "Taking Video Games to the Next Level," *Business Week*, May 9, 2005.

Global mobile entertainment: Arc Group.

Video streams: Accustream iMedia Research, January 26, 2005.

Text messages: Pete Lerma, "The Mobile Marketing Manifesto," www.clickz.com, May 3, 2005.

Video sales: Ross Johnson, "Video Sales are Good News in Hollywood. Shhh," *The New York Times*, January 31, 2005.

Television advertising: Saul Hansell, "More People Turn to the Web to Watch TV," *The New York Times*, August 1, 2005.

Digital images: Dan Carp, Chairman and CEO Eastman Kodak, CTIA Trade Show, 2005.

Online retail: *The State of Retailing Online 8.0*, Forrester Research for Shop.org.

Ring tone sales: "Ring Tones Make Sweet Music for Record Labels," Reuters, June 24, 2005.

Google Image Search: Google media release, 2005.

World Internet population: Internet World Stats, Usage and Population Statistics.

eBay items: Diane Werts, "CNBC's Report on eBay is Not Quite a Winning Bid," *Baltimore Sun*, June 29, 2005.

Web pages: Kevin Kelly, "We Are the Web," *Wired*, August 2005.

MAKING THE WORLD A BETTER PLACE
WITH SISOMO

Page 134: Dr. Jeffery Sachs, director of the Millennium Project, references the 8 million deaths per year from poverty and disease, including 3 million malaria fatalities and the $7 bed net, in a media briefing prior to the G8 Summit, June 15, 2005.

Page 134: The number of mobile phone users in Africa is recorded in "Mobile Growth 'Fastest in Africa,'" BBC News, March 9, 2005.

Page 135: www.saatchi.com/innovation/

Page 136: Wikipedia profiles Intel co-founder Gordon Moore and ethernet inventor Bob Metcalfe.

Page 137: Columnist Nicholas D. Kristof points out selectiveness by the media in "All Ears for Tom Cruise, All Eyes on Brad Pitt," *The New York Times*, July 26, 2005.

Page 137: The number and potential of young people is discussed by Susan Gigli, "Children, Youth and Media Around the World: An Overview of Trends and Issues," prepared for UNICEF, 4th World Summit on Media for Children and Adolescents, April, 2004.

Page 138: www.one.org is the website of ONE: The Campaign to Make Poverty History.

Page 138: Bono challenges America in "Tech Steps Up to Back Bono," *Business Week Online*, June 15, 2005.

Page 138: The ONE campaign's "Hollywood and Heartland Unite for ONE Campaign" media release details the facts and figures of the advertising campaign on April 10, 2005; as well as in the media release "Viewpoint and 'One: The Campaign to Make Poverty History' Partner to Deliver One Billion Online Ads Leading up to the G8 Summit in July," June 15, 2005.

Page 158: The idea of "digital dividends" was developed by Stuart N. Brotman, "The Digital Dividends," *Technology Review*, March 2002.

Acknowledgement

This book has grown out of a *coup de foudre* of Mark Jechura, from our client Procter & Gamble, and Adam Gerber from Starcom MediaVest Group. They first articulated for us the huge potential of Sight, Sound and Motion and its intense relationship with the screen. It was Pam Zucker, also from Starcom MediaVest Group, and Adam who created the name sisomo during a hothouse session in London with P&G and Publicis Groupe agencies, including Saatchi & Saatchi and Leo Burnett.

Kevin Roberts

Published in the United States by powerHouse Books,
a division of powerHouse Cultural Entertainment, Inc.
68 Charlton Street, New York, NY 10014-4601
telephone 212 604 9074, fax 212 366 5247
e-mail: sisomo@powerHouseBooks.com
website: www.powerHouseBooks.com

First edition, 2005

Library of Congress Cataloging-in-Publication Data:

Roberts, Kevin, 1949–
    Sisomo : the future on screen/Kevin Roberts.
      p. cm.
    Includes bibliographical references and index.
    ISBN 1-57687-268-8 (pbk.)
      1. Relationship marketing. 2. Advertising. I. Title.

    HF5415.55.R624 2005
    658.8'342--dc22   2005049168

ISBN 1-57687-268-8

Produced by Saatchi & Saatchi
Art Direction: Derek Lockwood
Design: Kane McPherson
Design Associates: Andy Scarth, Brad Avison

Printing and binding by Midas Printing

A complete catalog of powerHouse Books and Limited Editions is available upon request; please call, write, or find Sight, Sound and Motion on our website.

10 9 8 7 6 5 4 3 2 1

Printed and bound in China